A WAY WITH WORDS

Advice from the TEDx frontline on how to cut the crap and deliver a **killer message** whatever the communication method

THEO KAPODISTRIAS

Rethink

First published in Great Britain in 2024
by Rethink Press (www.rethinkpress.com)

This book also goes out to everyone who has supported me along the way – through the many endeavours, adventures, voluntary activities and jobs – and to all of the people who've influenced my life's path.

To my family and friends, who listen to me complain, who laugh with me, who grab me for a coffee, and who talk and banter with me. You make every day fun and worthwhile. Thank you.

Contents

Foreword

I started my career in August of 2010 in Seattle, WA, working as a software engineer for a little company by the name of Amazon. You may have heard of it. I was placed onto a team that was responsible for the availability of Amazon.com, which translated to making sure customers always had the best, fastest and most stable experience. At the time, I knew a great deal about writing beautiful, resilient code, but as it turns out, that was only part of what my career had in store.

Within the year, I was tasked with writing a weekly email to Jeff Bezos – or Uncle Jeff, as we called him – explaining the ins and outs of every little thing that went wrong throughout the course of the week. He would come to respond to those weekly emails with one of three symbols: ':)', ':(', or the dreaded '?'. It was quite a harrowing task for a twenty-two-year-old, fresh out of university, and I can confidently say that I fumbled my way through the first few emails to him. It became abundantly clear in those early weeks that if I wanted to be successful in this role, I would need to break from the normal, introverted demeanour of the software engineer and expand my toolbelt to include efficient and effective communication. I'm pleased to say that I only received smiles from Uncle Jeff, and I still have a few of those emails floating around somewhere.

This early experience ingrained in me the importance of not only honing my craft, but also developing my ability to communicate. It is a skill that served me well time and again as I went on to work at Salesforce on the core product experience; and it became make or break when I took a leap and founded my own Silicon Valley start-up, where I served as founder and CTO for six and a half years.

I am sure many of you have an image in your mind's eye of the prototypical tech start-up, with a bunch of engineers hacking away on code till all hours, living on caffeine and adrenaline. You're not wrong; but what gets obfuscated in this image is everything else that goes into building a successful company from the ground up, be it tech or otherwise. In order to build a successful company, you also need to carefully craft an ethos, a culture and a vision, and all of these things stem from being able to clearly and concisely communicate. It is paramount to be able to precisely present to personnel, craft compelling company updates, and confidently close deals with customers. These skills are hard wrought, and elusive for far too many. I undoubtedly had a head start when I founded Gremlin, but I still spent hours poring over books, articles, tips and tricks. I wish I had had this book with me then.

It was not until years later, after growing Gremlin to $10MM+ in revenue and 100 employees, that I took my leave and moved to Hobart, Tasmania, where I had the good fortune of meeting Theo. We instantly connected over many things, including our shared value of good communication. From that, an enduring friendship was born. During my time in Hobart, I had the distinct pleasure of learning about Theo's experience of marrying his legal career with his passion for public speaking, first by presenting at local and international events, and eventually by sharing his gift with others through coaching, online courses and his podcast. The cherry on top, though, was getting to witness him perform as the executive director of TEDxHobart in 2023, where he diligently organised and curated an incredible array of speakers on the theme of curiosity – a concept that holds a special place in my heart as one of my core values. Not only did Theo serve as the host for the event, adroitly weaving one talk into the next, but he also painstakingly coached each of the speakers, helping them flesh out and polish their talks until each one shone brightly and contributed perfectly to a beautifully cohesive narrative.

This book is an encapsulation of the prowess Theo used to craft that cunningly curious TEDxHobart in 2023. It speaks to so many of the lessons he has learned and taught over the many years he has dedicated to practical communication, public speaking and presentation skills. I consider it a tried and true testament to his ability to take a message and distil it into something poignant and powerful. I am positive you will find the same in the pages that follow.

—Matthew 'Forni' Fornaciari

Engineer-turned-founder, consultant, advisor and investor

Introduction

This book is for the professionals out there who want to be noticed and recognised. Maybe you're in a big organisation or a government department, and you're comfortable doing your thing, but you have ambition to do more.

What's stopping you from moving forward?

Do any of the following situations sound familiar?

- You feel uncomfortable speaking up at meetings because you don't feel what you have to say will be heard.
- You write emails to management and don't get the replies you want, or you sometimes don't even receive an acknowledgement.

- No one seems to listen to your ideas and contributions, and other people get the credit for your inputs?

It's bullshit, hey? Why don't you get this recognition?

What about a situation like this:

You find yourself sitting at your desk, when an email pops up. You think, *Uh, what?* You've just found out that the other guy in your team has been promoted to a senior position – one that wasn't advertised or discussed. Suddenly, Kevin is going to be paid at least $20,000 more per year.

Kevin stands out because he's a smooth talker. He knows how to get a message across, how to present in the boardroom, and how to write a decent email. The bastard!

I've been there. I started my career, at the age of twenty-three, as the junior in-house lawyer amongst a much older contingent. I was basically invisible. I didn't feel that there was a lot of respect for me or that I was respected for my opinion. I didn't feel like anyone in my team or the rest of the business listened to what I was saying.

If you're anything like me during that time:

- You want to build your influence at work, but you don't want to do something questionable or be a show-off.

- You want to be able to stand up in those team meetings and show your boss you know what you're talking about and that you're ready for a new challenge.
- You want to send a powerful email and get the approval you want, without receiving comments like, 'We need further clarification here', 'Look, I just don't understand what you're looking for', or the dreaded silence.

What I'm saying is: I get it. I also have some good news for you: it doesn't need to be this way forever.

I'm now a multinational award-winning lawyer, having been featured in national and global publications, radio programmes and podcasts, and on stages around the world. I went from being the reliable paper pusher, sitting in the corner, quietly doing my tasks, to becoming the general counsel (and sole legal officer) for global organisations. Through all of this, I also started my own business as a keynote speaker, trainer, MC, adviser and coach, to help people to speak up, show up and make an impact. Outside of being a lawyer, I'm the executive director (lead organiser and doer of things) of TEDxHobart. I'm also part of the TEDxHobart speaker coaching team, supporting people in going from shy and timid to global superstar. These days, I pull together all my skills from the professional world, the speaking world and the TEDx world to make people the success stories they want to be.

Communication can be a challenge. Public speaking can be hard, and not being amazing at it might be hurting your chances of moving forward.

I discovered what I needed to do to become influential with my voice. I learned how to speak up and communicate in a way to be listened to. I want to help you do the same.

Let's deal with all of the Kevins out there and be better than them. I've written this book because I have a bold vision to help those who feel they're stuck, just like I felt when I was younger.

Wouldn't it be amazing for you to be able to walk into the boardroom and feel confident, happy and pumped to get up and present to everyone?

Wouldn't it be the dream to not lay awake anxious because you don't know how to handle a challenging conversation at work?

Wouldn't it make life easier to be able to structure a report so that everyone knows how bloody smart you are?

This could be a reality.

I want to give you the tools to improve your verbal communication and your written communication, to enable you to be the champion you want to be. By the time you've finished this book, you'll feel more capable, confident and able to stand up and speak out. You will feel that you're being listened to because you're delivering the right message that the right people need to hear. After following my methods, you'll start to become known as the go-to person. You'll start to be considered for opportunities you didn't know existed. Your voice will be heard.

I'll take you through my 5C methodology for crafting and delivering messages that matter. This methodology covers the critical concepts you'll need to get your head around to allow you to take the lead, be the best and make sure everyone knows you have something to say. The 5Cs stand for:

- Clarity
- Conciseness
- Confidence
- Creativity
- Connection

You'll see that these 5Cs are the titles for the five parts of this book. As you work through them, you'll hear from other people who have been able to improve in these spaces and what that's meant for them. You'll get case studies, practical tips and checklists, and other awesome shit to ensure that you've got this.

PART ONE
CLARITY

When you're clear on who you're talking to, everything else becomes easy. Your audience members are the most important people for your communication. If you aren't considering those who are listening to you and reading your material, why are you bothering?

This part of the book delves into the clarity you need to understand about your audience and what will make them want to keep engaged with you. We'll explore:

- Models that can be implemented to ensure you capture your audience
- The voice you should be speaking in to reach your audience in the best possible way

ONE
Clarity Of Audience

Anytime you interact with someone, it's important to think about how they will receive the information. This isn't essentially about format – it's more about how the other person will interpret and understand what you're communicating. You might now be thinking, *If I send an email or say something to someone, it'll be pretty obvious what the hell I mean and what they will do with it.* That isn't necessarily the case, though.

Let's look at your workplace. You probably talk to twenty to thirty different people every day. Each interaction you have with those people is open to interpretation. Whether you're talking to Susan in accounting, Erin in human resources or Brodie in insurance, they're all different people, who have diverse levels of understanding, unique life experiences and different ways of comprehending information.

When you contact others in writing, you might be getting ignored or overlooked because you're not clear on what your reader wants to hear or how much of what you say they really understand.

How well do you know the person you're liaising with?

We are going to get clear on and look at why it's so important to find clarity in your audience, and we'll dig into some techniques to help you along the way.

In this chapter we're going to:

- Look at how critical it is to fully understand the person you are communicating with
- Make you think about the types of people you speak with

I'm keen to show you how you can impress your boss and your clients by connecting with them in new and impressive ways, because they know you get it.

This will put you above Kevin.

Let's do this.

Who are you talking to?

It's a typical day in the office. You've got your coffee in hand, and you're docking your laptop so you can get started with work. You check your emails, and you can see you've been asked similar questions from a few different people around the business. You might well be thinking, *Well, I can knock a few of these out in one go – ha!*

For efficiency, maybe that's a nice a simple way for you to clear out some bullshit and to continue with your day pushing more shit out. However, you might end up creating *more* work for yourself. Let me explain.

For the sake of this conversation, let's say you're in the financial team at a large company. Three people have asked you similar questions about GST (goods and services tax, for those not in Australia). You've decided that you'll create one response, do a copy-and-paste, and send the same response off to all. What you haven't considered is that those people have varying levels of knowledge about the topic. For example, one of the recipients has absolutely no idea about anything GST-related so your response is only going to cause confusion and more questions. Maybe that person will even want to organise a meeting for clarification. You might then need to follow up after the meeting with an email, to explain everything that was discussed in the meeting.

Are you seeing the pile of poo you've created? I know you didn't want to or mean to, but it's like when you think it'll be a good idea to send your dog outside in the backyard to get some exercise, only for him to roll around in dirt and then make his way back into the house. It simply generates more mess and work for you do deal with. What seemed like a good idea – sending the dog outside to get some air so he stops wanting pats or sending the same email to three people about the same topic – has created more work.

It is essential to know the people you're talking to and to understand your audience.

How to understand your audience

I always find it an interesting task when I'm asked, as a lawyer, to provide advice to my clients. I could write for hours about a niche and weird area of law, but if I did that, I don't think anyone would really want to talk to me.

Soon after I started working as a lawyer for an educational institution at the youthful age of twenty-three, I received an email from an associate professor. It was about an arrangement where he had gained a small funding grant for research and wanted to engage a number of experts to assist him in completing the work. I remember receiving the email and thinking that it would be important for me to make a good impression and sound smart. I compiled an email full of guidance for the professor, and I wanted it to sound like it came from a lawyer. Now that I had that title, I wanted to use it.

Well, that wasn't a great idea.

My phone rang, and it was my old mate, the associate professor. I picked up, and he said, 'Who the *hell* do you think you are? I've worked here for twenty years, and I'm not going to be spoken down to by someone who got lost at the university on the way to high school.'

Um... rude.

It was a useful lesson, though. It made me realise that my legal advice, and the way I explained the steps ahead, were way too complicated and confusing. My email wasn't designed for someone who is proficient in the academic space but not equipped in the legal space. I should have thought about the person I was talking to and then how I could best serve them. I needed to better understand my audience and how I would speak with them.

One way you can be recognised for your brilliance is when people feel you're talking directly to them. When you speak someone's language, they'll feel more connected with you.

There are many circumstances where you have to talk to bigger groups of people where you don't know everyone, for example, when you're presenting at a conference or creating a bulk email or a poster. You then don't have the luxury of knowing how much your audience will understand or how all of the various people will hear what you're saying. There are ways to make your voice heard amongst all of those people, though, and for your messages to have real impact, even if you don't yet have clarity on who you're speaking to. Key here is to speak clearly and plainly, to ensure that the wider world knows what you mean.

TWO EXAMPLES OF COMMUNICATING WITH A MASS AUDIENCE

If you're in Australia, you may remember receiving the following text message in March 2020:

> 'Coronavirus Aus Gov msg: To stop the spread, stay 1.5m from others, follow rules on social gatherings, wash hands, stay home if sick. aus.gov.au'

The New Zealand government sent a warning text message around the same time:

> 'This message is for all of New Zealand. We are depending on you. Follow the rules and STAY HOME. Act as if you have COVID-19. This will save lives. Remember:
>
> Where you stay tonight is where YOU MUST stay from now on.

> You must only be in physical contact with those you are living with.
>
> It is likely Level 4 measures will stay in place for a number of weeks.
>
> Let's all do our bit to unite against COVID-19.
>
> Kia kaha.'

When you compare these messages, which one is easier to understand? Which one feels like it's speaking to you?

When I've asked this question at conferences and events, using these texts as examples, the overwhelming response is that the New Zealand message is waaaaay better.

Why is that?

In terms of having clarity on their audiences, neither government knows every single person they are speaking with. It is hard to cater communication to such a wide group of people and for it to land. Bluntly, though, the Australian text message sucks.

This isn't about any political leanings or other bias. It's just me, as a dude who knows how to have interactions and knows about communication, saying that the text message fails in a few ways:

- It feels impersonal. There's no human feel to the message; it's only a brief list of five instructions.
- It expects me to know what '1.5m' is. I can take a pretty good guess, but will everyone – all 26 million (or so) people in Australia – know that the 'm' refers to metres?

- It assumes I know what is meant by 'stop the spread'. Of course, I can read between the lines to know that it's referring to stopping the spread of that little thing called COVID, but if you're trying to get a point across to so many people, you shouldn't assume they know what you're talking about. Similarly, the message expects everyone, at the start of the pandemic, to know the rules on social gatherings.

Meanwhile, the New Zealand message does some pretty awesome things. Here's why it works so well:

- It feels personal, as if it was written to me personally, and I kinda like being spoken to as an individual.
- It's in a language I can understand and that most people can understand.

It speaks in a way that we can relate to, using clear examples and ways of thinking such as 'Act as if you have COVID-19'. If I was a reasonable person and not a complete anus, on reading that message, I'd assume that means that I should stay isolated in my home.

As mentioned before, it's vital to speak in the language of the people reading or listening to your communications. Keep this in mind for down the track – we'll be talking about it more in Chapter Two.

What do they need to know?

Understanding who you're communicating with will allow you to tailor what you're saying, because you understand more about their particular needs. When you have this understanding, it's also key to think about what the person you're speaking to actually needs to know.

Let's go back to that example I used earlier, where you've been asked that question about GST. Instead of sending out a generic response to everyone, let's start to examine each person, the section of the business they're in, and why they may be asking the question.

It doesn't hurt to sit in their shoes and think about things from their perspective. A few questions that'll help get your mind rolling:

- How much do they know about the topic? Is it something that might be new to them or do they already have some knowledge about it?
- Is this a pivotal opportunity for you to show what you're talking about and how useful you could be?
- How can you deliver this information in a way that is going to be most effective, based on what you know? (I'll cover more on format and creativity in Chapter Seven.)

All of this might sound like a lot of work, and you may at first spend more time thinking about how to communicate than on the communication itself.

Ultimately, though, you'll become awesome at this because you'll use this mode of thinking on the regular.

Putting this into practice – thinking about what people really want to know – is only going to propel you further. Pairing that with knowing who you're speaking with, and communicating in a language and format they understand, will make you their go-to person in your area of expertise. Can you imagine being the legendary champion that everyone – both colleagues and clients – looks up to as the genius who makes complex things seem so simple to understand? The person who speaks to others as if they're human? Someone who does all of this work and perfectly sums up everything they need to know?

This is all in the realm of reality. Keep that in mind as you read on, because this is the opportunity for you to build yourself up and position yourself in the best light for future growth potential. Who knows – your improved communication could even lead to a promotion, a new job or a big-ass project that shines the national spotlight on you.

Let's think about an example a lot of us would be pretty familiar with. Have you ever received a message, likely on Facebook, that reads something like this?

> Hey bro/hun, I was looking at your profile
> and couldn't help but notice how awesome
> you are. I've got an amazing opportunity,

> which may or may not be for you, but I just need to tell you about it! I've got three places available for a business opportunity, where you could earn up to $5,000 a month extra in the pockets of free time you have, all while working from home. It's so simple – you need to message everyone you know and sell some basic products everyone needs such as shampoo. It's basically you making money in your own time without leaving the couch. Do you want to be your own boss? D'you wanna earn that little bit more to make life that much more comfortable? Let me know.

Yes – it's multi-level marketing, also known as MLM, direct sales or the classic pyramid schemes (noting that a pyramid scheme is slightly different, but they sometimes all get bundled in the same bucket).

Reading that message, you might think, *What is this shit?* or *Why would I want to even read this, let alone apply?* Those reactions are completely justified. I always giggle a little when I receive one of these messages – experience tells me the job would need me to ostracise my friends and family by pestering them to become salespeople for me, and I couldn't think of anything worse. The message doesn't work on me in selling the 'dream' of working from home, and the extra money per month isn't particularly enticing as messages like this provide more promise than they can actually deliver. It also doesn't explain everything I'd want to know – I have no idea about how I would be making the money. It is in fact almost certain I would need to find people to sell under me, or that making money means I need to send a message to everyone I know, trying to convince them too that this is a good idea. I know better. However, this person or company is not aiming for a defined target audience. They're using the scatter-gun approach: send everyone a message and see what happens.

One of the earliest examples of this approach came from Tupperware. Some housewives, who were home looking after their little ones, felt lonely and wanted to embark on a new hobby. The title of Madeleine Morley's 2019 article says it all: 'Tupperware Was the Original Social Network of 1950s Suburbia'. It made sense back then – housewives could socialise by throwing Tupperware parties, while also earning some income.

For the people multi-level marketers want to target, the approach works – the people who are financially struggling might think that this is a get-rich-quick scheme and the answer to their needs. They feel they are being spoken to – someone is whispering in their ear, and they're going to jump at the opportunity. For that group of people, the MLMer understands their audience and has clarity on who they're speaking with, offering a supposedly great and convenient way to make a new income.

My Facebook profile is pretty private (other than my public 'like' page, which is open and promotes my business activity). If a multi-level marketer looked at my profile and saw that I was a lawyer, they probably wouldn't approach me directly, particularly not with a 'Hey bro/hun', as that isn't how I generally talk. Lawyers will research everything – no stone left unturned – so we would do our research and realise the message above wasn't relevant for us. I would discover all sorts of information to explain why it wouldn't work for me or why I wouldn't be interested, and I would most likely block the person who sent me a message.

The lesson here: once you have clarity on who you're speaking with, you can craft a message that matters to them, which makes it a lot easier to be heard by your listener. You want to be a person of influence.

What's the ultimate goal from this?

I'll cut the bullshit and lay it out for you as simply as I can: once you get a clear idea of who you're speaking with and what they need to know, you will have the launchpad to really shine.

You now need to consider two new perspectives:

1. What is the ultimate goal for the person you're communicating with?
2. What is *your* goal from this communication?

It's important to understand that person's goal – their reason for listening to you – as this will be an important factor in how you craft your explanation. For example, does the person you're communicating with need to make a decision which could have major financial implications? Is it about where someone should go for dinner? Or are you presenting to a group of people who do not understand the topic, and you want to educate them?

As we've looked at in detail in this chapter, having clarity on your audience will provide you with the platform for success. (This is something Kevin is probably great at doing, the annoying bastard.) If the goal for your audience is also clear, it makes your job much easier.

Considering the COVID text message examples from earlier: the goal, to be achieved by the audience, is for communities to stay safe and not get infested with the spicy cough. That's a pretty great goal. However, it is questionable whether the people drafting the Australian message had the audience in mind as they created it. It wasn't totally clear, and it used ambiguous terms. With the New Zealand text message, the audience was clearly in mind – it was written in a way for people to understand what they needed to do. The goal for the people they were communicating with was to keep safe. The goal for the New Zealand government was to instruct people on how to comply and remain safe, and to prevent the spread of the disease.

I'd like you to focus a little on yourself, answering the second question above: What is *your* goal from this communication? Sometimes a great email or an awesome presentation can be used as an example, by which people say, 'Geez – Bryan is clever, hey?' or 'Shit – didn't know Kelly was so knowledgeable on this'. In short: when you get clarity on your audience and their goal, it could benefit you too. You'll therefore also have a goal from all of this, and that's OK. I want you to become the master of your own domain – the baddest babe/bro/human there ever was. You want to be recognised for those job opportunities. You want to appear confident, to smash others and to get noticed. Let's never forget what can be achieved through powerful communication.

Summary

This chapter has given you the first step in communicating your value to ensure your voice is heard.

I've highlighted the importance of having clarity about your audience, knowing exactly who they are and what they do. The more clarity you have, the easier if will be for you to understand what they need to get from your communication.

If you are speaking to a large audience and don't know everyone, speaking in a clear and plain way will ensure everyone understands your message.

Think about the goals of your audience as well as your own goal. Why are they speaking with you? Why do they want information? What can you achieve from the communication that reflects positively on you?

These are some key skills to get your head around. Take them with you as we move to the next phase of having clarity in your voice and the ability to understand your circumstances.

TWO
Clarity Of Voice

If you've googled me, and from what you've already gathered from this book, you'll know I love TED and the TEDx franchises. I am also involved in organising TEDx events. The now world-renowned TEDx speaker Brené Brown explains in her book, *Dare to Lead,* that 'Clear is kind'. She talks about this in the context of leadership development, but this next excerpt from her book may ring true for you too:

> 'I first heard this saying (Clear is kind. Unclear is unkind.) two decades ago in a twelve-step meeting, but I was on slogan overload at the time and didn't even think about it again until I saw the data about how most of us avoid clarity because we tell ourselves that we're

> being kind, when what we're actually doing is being unkind and unfair.
>
> Feeding people half-truths or bullshit to make them feel better (which is almost always about making ourselves feel more comfortable) is unkind.'

Being clear about what you're saying will help you tremendously, because you'll only ever have to say it once. It will also help the people you're communicating with, because they'll understand it and it'll be useful for them. In this chapter, we're going to explore some of those important communication tactics of gaining clarity of voice and of plain English principles.

We're going to take a dive into what I call the Clarity Triangle, which comprises three key elements:

1. Audience
2. Context
3. Content

Having covered the first point, in this chapter we're going to explore the other two points of the Clarity Triangle.

I want you to be able to walk into any room, into any situation, knowing you'll be listened to and recognised as the damn best that room has ever seen. When you've mastered having a clear voice and producing clear communications, you will have ticked off a significant milestone. Conquering this next step is going to be huge.

The Clarity Triangle

Because it's so important, I want to reiterate: having clarity prior to communicating with others is going to get you far in your communication journey. Having a significantly better understanding of your audience and their needs will take you to the next level up compared with everyone else.

The three vital factors that give you clarity in your communications are:

1. **Audience:** As covered in Chapter One, this is about gaining clarity on who you are talking to, what they need to know, and their goal in listening to you.

2. **Context:** Here you need to recognise the context of the communication. What is the background? Why are you engaging in this discussion? This will help you determine the best way to communicate and whether you need to do anything in particular to make it work.

   As an example: if the communication is in a work context, you should consider which department the person works in, and the specific issues and needs of the people in that department.

3. **Content:** This is about creating the content for your presentation, report or email, or any other form of communication, based on your audience and the context.

   Including tailored and specific information that is in context and relevant for your audience will make it far more engaging and useful for those engaging with the content.

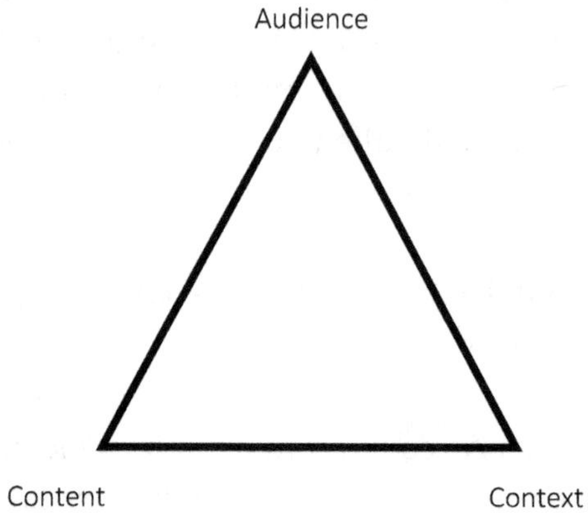

The Clarity Triangle

Getting the context right

It can be easy to misunderstand or make assumptions about circumstances, and we sometimes don't realise that we may be deep in a conflict. I'm not sure how many times I've blindly walked into the kitchenette of my workplace (past ones, mind you) and said an enthusiastic 'Oh, hey!', only then to find that the two people already in the kitchenette are bickering about something. Awkward! How to manage this tight spot?

Let's think about Kevin in this type of situation – the dashing, well-spoken and overtly confident Kevin, who can apparently do no wrong. He's able to be so successful because he knows who he is talking to. Whether it's a client or a work colleague, he knows how to position his communications to suit them. He understands the context – why he's being asked to do it, where this all fits into the bigger picture and what he is expected to do. He also knows the circumstances, including the politics around the situation. He gets that there are a few tensions to deal with. Hey, Kevin was brought in as an independent person to change the mood.

Kevin might be an annoying bastard, but he's an annoying bastard who knows how to communicate well. With the Clarity Triangle, you can too.

When I think about the Clarity Triangle, the context part always rings as being the glue that binds everything together. The context determines many things, including:

- The occasion
- The entire purpose of your communication
- How you're meant to prepare for the presentation or the piece you're writing
- The expectations of the audience, given the context and setting they're in

As an example, let's say you've been given a guest appearance on a kids' educational show. The main presenter is playing with a teddy bear and telling the audience about how it needs to go and play with the other teddies that are sitting nearby. You then decide to cause a ruckus. You get the toy fire truck, drive over the other teddies and say that they're now dead. This would of course be horrendous for the children watching, and for their parents, who would have to deal with a plethora of questions. It's completely out of context and therefore inappropriate.

I know – it's a bit of a wild example, but let's keep going with it. Instead of wanting to kill the other teddies, something that would be a little (or a lot) more appropriate would be to ask, 'Why don't we take this teddy to his friends by riding on the fire truck?' That would be in context and therefore appropriate for the audience, the story and the entire programme.

If the context isn't necessarily that obvious, it's worth asking yourself – or others who have more knowledge – about the communication opportunity. Try using the following questions as a guide:

1. What is the overall purpose of the communication?

   For example, you might have been asked to inform the team about a project you're working on, or you might be presenting at an industry event about the hottest new trend in your space. This question will help you determine the type of content you'll share and the sorts of things to discuss.

2. When and where will this occur?

   The occasion and situation is important to consider as they will influence the format you'll use to deliver your information and how you need to present yourself, including what you should wear.

3. How much detail is appropriate for this audience and environment?

   Based on the type of presentation or written work you're producing, you need to know how much information makes sense for this type of crowd.

4. Are there particular constraints and guidelines I need to follow?

   There could be company guidelines and branding requirements, or you may need to follow a particular template to present the information.

5. Is there stuff I shouldn't mention or that would make any of the audience uncomfortable?

   There could, for example, be controversial things occurring in the media or things related to your audience that you need to avoid completely.

Background work to determine and consider context will allow you to properly prepare and will make your communication more robust.

Preparation is equally important when it comes to your content. The content you share is the guts of your communication. Later in this book, you'll find detail on different types of content, including stories, facts, figures and statistics, and the best ways to use all those. Creating a tailored experience for your audience will make a big difference when you understand the environment in which you're presenting. In this chapter I'll focus on how you can keep you communication as clear and structured as possible.

Plain English principles

Perhaps the greatest tool in your communication toolkit is plain English.

In her book *Clear and Concise*, Susan McKerihan clarifies, 'Plain English is clear, concise language that uses the right words in the right place. Its objective is to ensure that the intended reader understands the message quickly and accurately.'

It's crucial to understand that plain English isn't about dumbing down what you're saying. You can use technical or specialist language where required and discuss complex subjects, but these can still be expressed in plain English. The objective is simple: speaking and writing in plain English enables your audience to focus on the message rather than be distracted by difficult language or complicated sentences. The benefit for you, as the person presenting the information, is that you'll be viewed not only as an expert in this topic but also as someone skilled in explaining complex messages clearly.

Lucy McCarraher and Joe Gregory explain in their book, *Bookbuilder*:

> 'If there's a hard way or an easy way to say something, use the easy way. If there's a long way or a short way to describe something, take the short route.... Do your readers a favour by not assuming they have your level of knowledge – they are reading your book precisely because they don't.'

The same can be applied to all forms of communication. If you're presenting to a room full of people, the audience is there to learn and obtain new knowledge. Using plain English to explain things in the clearest way possible will ensure that your audience are being considered throughout the whole process.

I'll run through some key principles, for you to consider and keep in your back pocket, ready for every time you communicate. Buckle in – we're going for an adventure.

1. Remove useless words

As highlighted by the title of this chapter, an important characteristic of good communication is clarity. When trying to be clear, we sometimes end up saying way more than we need. Here's an example:

'Should you wish to discuss anything further, or if you need any additional information, please don't hesitate to contact me at any time.'

Instead, you could simply say:

'Please contact me if you have questions or need further information.'

What can we do to deal with this issue? McKerihan outlines a few things we need to avoid:

- **Unnecessary qualifiers:** We often add words that don't change the meaning or give emphasis. For example, 'an explanatory introduction' can just be 'an introduction'; 'you basically need to' is better as simply 'you need to'.
- **Wordy phrases:** We often use a bundle of words where it's clearer to use a few. For example, instead of 'at the end of the day', use 'ultimately'; instead of 'I would be very grateful if you could', use 'Please'.
- **There is / there are:** These starters don't change or add anything to the sentence. For example, 'There

are a number of references used in this book that relate to Australia' could instead be 'A number of references used in this book relate to Australia'.

- **Repetition:** We often don't notice when we repeat words, phrases or ideas, but this can be confusing or boring for the person we're engaging with.
- **Throat clearers:** These are redundant terms that people use to start a sentence, out of habit or due to hesitation. While the speaker likely doesn't even notice they're using, the listener will likely be distracted, and they'll be less impressed by your core messages. Some examples: 'It goes without saying that…', 'It is important to remember that…', 'Basically, considering everything involved…'. If you removed those introductions from any sentence, no sense or emphasis is lost.

2. Use everyday words

People usually think that they will sound smarter if they use big, fancy-sounding words. Almost always, the opposite is true. Using long words will generally piss people off – the words only provide a distraction and make it harder for people to follow what you're telling them. As a confident communicator, using everyday and familiar language will demonstrate that you know your topic and content so well that you can explain it in a way that can be understood by anyone, without feeling the need to impress them with your vocabulary.

When we write, we tend to articulate content in a formal way, very differently from how we speak. To see if something you've written is in plain English, try reading it out loud. Does it sound human? Or can you make the wording sound more relaxed and natural?

In the business world, people often use abstract words, describing intangible concepts and attitudes, for example 'integrity' and 'efficiency'. While those words are sometimes necessary in a business context, they can be annoying if overused. Your content will be clearer if you:

- Use concrete, factual words
- Explain clearly what you mean
- Give real-life examples of what you are describing

3. Avoid ambiguity

When things are ambiguous, it can be very hard for someone to follow what's going on. There is something in this space that drives me up the wall: unclear pronoun references. For example, I have a friend who is a childcare worker, and she'll regularly share stories such as this one:

> 'I was assigned a young girl to look after and, in the afternoon, she was joined by her cousin. The girls both wanted to go to the park, so we went. She started pulling her hair and the

> other started screaming. She said, 'I hate the park' and then the other said, 'Yeah – why are we here?' You just can't win.'

I have no idea in this context who 'she' is. Both persons in the story were young women, so when referencing 'she' and 'her', it needs to be obvious which one is being talking about.

Pronouns are used to replace nouns, whether referring to people or things. If it is unclear which person or thing the pronoun is replacing, the listener or reader will be confused. In case of any potential uncertainty, it makes more sense to use the full reference and name rather than unclear pronoun references.

I'll be talking about plain English a lot throughout this book, as it's such an important topic for public speaking, presentations and communication in general. When it's used well, it can make a world of difference. Plain English helps you to connect with others and bring them on the journey with you, and to connect them with your message and the value you provide.

Presentation structure guide

When you are preparing a presentation, it can feel hard to know where to start, but I want to introduce you to a tool I created for structuring a presentation. This will assist you in planning your talk, and it will also introduce you to some of the important points

I raise later in the book. I've created a model that you'll find at end of this chapter which will help you visualise this presentation structure. Following this structure will make your life easier and your presentation first-class:

- Introduction
- Body – three key points
- Conclusion

Before we discuss the structure in detail, let's talk about timing. For a thirty-minute presentation, for example, the timing would be something like this:

- Introduction – three minutes
- Body – three key points – seven minutes each
- Conclusion – three minutes

This will leave you with a few spare minutes at the end, in case you need the extra time or for some questions from the audience.

Introduction

This is where you gain the attention of your audience – it's the opportunity to captivate them from the start. Ideally, kick things off with a bold statement about the topic. This grabs everyone's attention, hooking them in early on and making them interested in what you'll say next. Obviously, the type and format of that bold statement will depend on the presentation you're giving. It could be a quote, a short anecdote, or a surprising or shocking statement, to make everyone's ears prick up.

The introduction is also your chance to set the agenda and broadly outline the main things you'll be covering. Start by building off the bold statement you've made, setting the scene and context for your talk, which will allow you to settle into the more detailed content to follow.

Body – three key points

This is the chunky part. It's where you throw in all that awesome value you provide – your knowledge and expertise.

For each key point, it is important to include:

- Factual or statistical information, with evidence
- Stories and creative elements to entertain and help people remember
- Some conclusions on that key point

This book later digs into all of the above in more detail when considering creativity in communications and connecting with audiences through tailored communications. Note also the discussion in Chapter Nine on content focused on the left brain and right brain.

Conclusion

This is an important aspect for your big finish. It's the opportunity to do a bit of a recap on everything you've spoken about and to bring home that main message you've wanted to get across. The conclusion is where you can reinforce key points, ensuring that your audience walks away remembering the most important things.

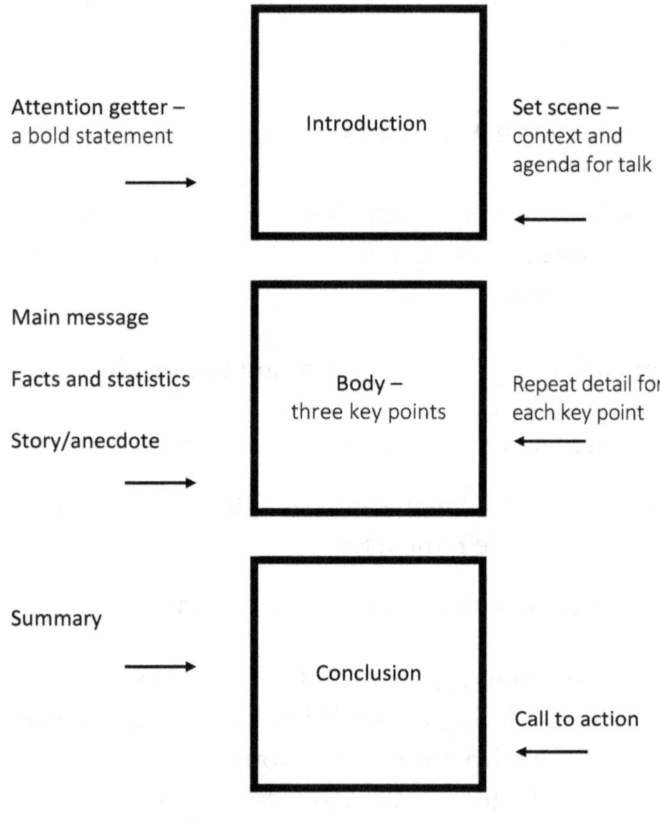

Presentation structure guide

The conclusion is also the place where you can provide a call to action, encouraging your audience members to do something. That could be to change a particular behaviour or to do something specific.

Summary

The clarity of voice is about being clear with your words, what you're saying and how you're saying it. My Clarity Triangle provides the guidance and support to frame how communications need to be presented and can help with knowing the best way to share the message. Understanding your audience remains key. From that, knowing the appropriate context will make it easy for you to know what is and isn't OK to share. Finally, completing the triangle is having the right content in place to reach the hearts and minds of your audience.

The use of plain English is the most critical thing in your toolkit to create accessible and easy-to-understand messages. The power of giving people something they don't need to think too hard about means your message will resonate, and it will make listening to you a breeze. My presentation structure guide helps to give you a useful structure for creating any type of presentation, ensuring you can get your message out to your audiences.

PART TWO
CONCISENESS

Time is a precious commodity, so being concise is a critical principle of communication. You don't want to waste time or fill it for the sake of occupying space.

You only have seven seconds to make a positive first impression. You want to use your time with your audience wisely.

This part of the book runs through the principle of being concise and provides a range of practical mechanisms. We'll consider the means of being succinct and improving the pull you can have every time you communicate, regardless of the format of that communication.

THREE

Conciseness: Too Long, Didn't Read

One of the best things you can learn in the art and science of communication is the ability to find the balance between giving a lot but not too much. Knowing the right amount of detail, providing enough context and saying just enough can be an incredibly powerful skill.

It can be tricky to be concise. I'll run through some key examples and illustrate techniques that will ensure that every time you speak or every time you communicate, you'll be doing so in a powerful and succinct way.

One thing I always think about is how horrendous and stressful it is to receive something that has way too much text. Trying to read it all can do something to your brain, and it isn't a fun experience. Even worse is if you have to listen to something long and draining – you don't take that information in. Think back to those classes at school or those lectures at university that felt like they were never going to end. You don't want your audience to ever feel like that.

This chapter will explore why too much information can be painful. This is not only when there's too much detail but also when there's just way too much information – as the kids say: TMI (too much info).

The modern brain

Trying to get people's attention is hard. Trying to maintain someone's attention is even more difficult.

I'm not sure about you, but I really enjoy settling into my couch, fully charged phone in hand, and scrolling through TikTok, Instagram and even LinkedIn (if I'm feeling corporate).

The joy of platforms like TikTok is that the content is short enough to grab your attention, and if something doesn't appeal, you can scroll away until you find something fun and entertaining again. Anna Lembke, MC psychiatry professor and Chief of the Addiction Medicine Dual Diagnosis at Stanford University explains that social media is the 'bottomless bowl' where we see 'flashing lights, rankings and images and videos of attractive people where our brains release more dopamine than it may with typical real-life interactions' (as per McNamara in *teenVogue*). The more you see things that you enjoy through social media, the more you begin to crave it. In the same article, Tristan Harris, Co-Founder and President of the Centre for Humane Technology, explains that social media is similar to slot machines – although you don't know how positive the interaction will be, it *might* be. You're gambling on the outcome and switch on the social media apps in the hopes of having a good time.

Our phones and the internet constantly provide us with so much information that our brains can get overloaded. Cognitive overload refers to the state in which the amount of information presented to us exceeds our cognitive processing capacity. With all the potential information out there – including social media, news, emails, texts, online communication platforms – our brains are constantly bombarded with more data and information than we can reasonably handle.

When we're exposed to such excessive levels of information, our attention span decreases. While people are becoming hard-wired to enjoy things that are fun and entertaining in the first three seconds, it can of course be hard to grab and maintain the attention of people we're communicating with.

Every time you communicate with your customers, clients, partners and friends, if you're considered boring or not worth listening to, this will significantly affect those people's judgement on how valuable and beneficial you are as a provider of information and service. Sharing too much dense information will not have the effect you want it too. You'll over-face and put off people you're trying to impress.

We will explore the power of being concise in how we communicate, as it can have a huge impact on how people listen and consider what we're sharing and their ability to hold onto that information and use it. After all, what's the point in sharing anything if it isn't going to be used?

Too much to handle

Imagine this: you're sitting at a conference, and the presenter starts shouting out a heap of content – a never-ending flood of words. The slides on screen are filled to the brim with words in a tiny font size, just so the presenter could fit even more words in. Your brain reacts. You either start reading everything on the screen and stop listening, or you think, *Ughhhh... I'll just go and check Instagram for a minute and pretend this presentation isn't even happening.*

Research in cognitive neuroscience and psychology talks about processing fluency, the ease with which information is processed by the brain. How quickly people can understand and mentally process information presented to them will determine their judgements on that information.

In their article 'If It's Hard to Read, It's Hard to Do', Hyunjin Song and Norbert Schwarz explain:

> 'People are more likely to engage in a given behaviour the less effort it requires. As numerous studies have indicated, high perceived effort is a major impediment to behaviour change, from adopting an exercise routine (eg DuCharme and Brawley, 1995) to changing one's diet (eg Sparks, Guthrie, and Shepherd, 1997).'

If you present information in convoluted ways, using confusing language, big blocks of text, or just a bundle of information that isn't easy to comprehend, people will ignore the content or actively choose not to engage with it. If you want to grab people's attention and encourage them to do things, your communication needs to be easy to follow and understand.

It'll sound obvious when I say this, but you do not want to make things harder than necessary for people. In the study by Song and Schwarz, they used printed instructions with hard-to-read fonts, which made people assume the actions themselves would also be difficult. If you provide too much detail, perhaps in an attempt to show people how much you know, it's more likely they will switch off. Similarly, if you include lots of text, complicated PowerPoint presentations or language that is difficult to understand, no one will bother doing anything with that information.

This reminds me of my early days as a lawyer, when I'd try and show how smart I was with all of my research and information, when all my client wanted was a straightforward answer to their question. Below is one example of messy language and confusing presentation of information making everyone ignore what was being said.

CASE STUDY: 'I do not understand' – being too technical

Early in my career, I was working as a corporate lawyer, and I didn't receive administrative support. Being a lawyer often isn't as glamourous as the movies make it out to be. It involves a lot of paperwork and other stuff that needs to be read. *Yawn*, you might be thinking. Well, yeah.

As a side note: I'm terrible at a lot of administrative work. Put me in client meetings, let me chat to people, give me fun projects where I can learn something new, and I'm on fire. If I have to sit still and file emails away, make sure all signed documents are filed in the right place and ensure all notes are tucked away in the right folder... I'm sorry, but this kills me. I feel my insides melting at the thought. You want to make my soul burn? Give me a pile of administrative tasks.

While I was working in that job, I received an email from someone in the Records Management Unit – the team that managed the digital database, which housed all records for the business. It would have been a horrible job for me, but they all enjoyed it, and I liked talking with them – a nice bunch of people.

I clicked on the email from the very lovely records person – we'll call them Gwen – and my eyes glazed over. There were so many words, many of which I'd never heard before. I couldn't understand it. I just kept rereading the email, and it didn't become any clearer. It was filled with technical language – about 'disposal schedules', 'record types', 'folder positions and sub-folder structures', 'archival procedures' – it just kept going. All I saw was a big block of text that didn't appear to have a main point and continued spouting information. I closed the email and continued on with my life. I had to simply ignore it.

Later that day, I had a team meeting with the other lawyers. Someone asked, 'Did anyone else receive the email from Gwen?' and, in unison, everyone groaned 'Yeah…'

'I just deleted it. I couldn't understand her,' said one lawyer.

'I didn't feel like it was for me as it was too hard to understand so assumed it was sent by mistake,' said another.

Guess I'm not the only one who sucks at administrative tasks. Everyone in the room had concluded the email probably wasn't something we needed to worry about because it didn't make sense to us. We had reached cognitive overload.

When information is clear and concise, it reduces the cognitive load for those reading or listening. Gwen's email had caused the opposite reaction. As identified above, this is a case of processing fluency, where our minds went blank, and we decided that this wasn't important because it didn't make sense.

Finding the balance – concise principles

Communicating in a concise way and applying concise communication principles allows us to bring forward a message that is clear and presented in an easy-to-understand format.

Imagine this for a moment: you're in the office, and you have a question about a marketing campaign that is about to be launched. You head over and speak to the marketing coordinator to find out some information that's important for your job.

'Hey Janice, may I ask what some of the activities are for the marketing campaign?'

Janice slowly spins around in her chair, placing her floral coffee mug down on a coaster, which is stained and covered in biscuit crumbs. She says, 'Oh well, through Meta, we're going to drip a set of content and then lead to the gated content, which will allow for the "going live" component, which will direct users to the hamburger menu, where people will select their preferred sequence and then be sucked into the lead nurturing component…'

You look blankly at her, not sure of all the things she's said, say 'OK... great', and keep walking. Not only did Janice not exactly answer your question, but she also provided information that wasn't going to assist you.

Janice clearly needs to apply some of the following concise principles for a better result from her communication. They will also help you provide information in a concise way and demonstrate your credibility.

1. **Clarity**

   To condense a message, it is of utmost importance that you have a clear understanding of the topic and the audience you're speaking to. Before doing anything, apply the techniques from the earlier chapters and be clear on the entire purpose of this message you're sharing, who it's for, and the key takeaways for everyone involved. If you're creating a presentation, spending time at the start to map things out will save you hours upon hours of time. If you put a PowerPoint presentation together without doing any of the prep work, most of what you have compiled will go in the trash. We'll talk more about PowerPoint presentations and how to structure those later in the book.

2. **Key points**

   Not all information is created equal. You need to identify the core message and point you're trying to make, and stack those on top of the cake as a priority piece. Assess everything you want to say and order it using the 'triangle' approach (I love a triangle, by the way) – the most critical information comes first, at the tip of the triangle, followed by supporting details.

This method will enable you to capture the attention of your audience. If their attention fades, at the very least they'll remember the key points you provided and have the additional information you shared somewhere in the back of their mind.

3. **The right words**

   Due to people's limited attention spans, you need to share your message in the clearest form possible by choosing the best words to use. Every word should earn its place when you communicate. Use strong and descriptive words that convey the precise meaning or can create a visual impression so that your points get noticed and remembered.

4. **Brevity**

   When being concise, you should actually be concise, ya know? Embracing the concept of brevity allows you to convey the message in as few words as possible without sacrificing the clarity of the message. This is your ability to distil complex ideas into easily digestible nuggets of information. It's a hard skill but it comes with practice.

5. **The final edit**

   If you're speaking at an event, you'll be making notes in advance, so make sure you review and edit your content before the event. Critically review your work, applying the principles we've looked at. Consider if anything is too wordy, if you're using redundant words, or if your content is too technical for the people you're speaking with. Be critical and don't be afraid to make changes – we're all learning and growing, and communication is something we can all work on.

These principles will make a significant difference to how you speak, how you write and how you present information. If Janice applied these principles, any interaction she had would be powerful and effective, and I for one would have walked away better informed. Being able to refine your message does take a lot of practice, and some of the best communicators find this one of the most challenging skills to master. However, with patience and practice, you'll be able to hone these skills and communicate your message efficiently and effectively.

CASE STUDY: Why oversharing is bad

As I was planning this book, one story came to mind immediately as a 'what *not* to do'. During the pandemic, I decided I wanted to build a community and meet new people from the comfort of my home. A few of my friends had become a bit distant or retreated to a comfortable place, where they didn't want to socialise or engage in phone calls or any of that sort of stuff. For me, work was really challenging, especially due to a demanding new role, and I felt the need to connect with like-minded people.

In my search for new connections, I was invited to the beta testing environment of a new social audio app. The activity was described as 'live podcasting', where people would host conversations and anyone who shared an interest in the topic could listen or join in with the conversation. In the early days, many celebrities jumped on, and those conversations would attract thousands of people to listen to the celebs' pearls of wisdom. It was wild.

On this weird but sometimes wonderful app, I'd meet and chat with lots of people. I made some incredible friends on it, so it definitely brought some good things into my life, but it also brought some bizarre moments that I won't forget in a long time.

Giving people a platform – particularly people who may be feeling isolated – seems like a good idea in theory, yet the end result can be a bit of a challenge. I recall one conversation in particular where the group was having an interesting conversation when one person steered the topic to a difficult situation they had recently experienced, and they started to over-share. This resulted in the number of participants dropping quickly.

When you share too much detail, you can make other people feel uncomfortable. In this context, I refer to it as 'trauma dumping' – essentially sharing the traumatic details of your past almost as a means of receiving free therapy from a room of unqualified people.

In his book *TED Talks: The Official TED Guide to Public Speaking*, Chris Anderson, the head of TED Conferences, explains that it's important to find a balance between sharing too much and not enough, as you don't want every presentation to feel like a reality TV show. He says 'authentic vulnerability is powerful. Oversharing is not.' TED Talks rules also stipulate that talks must last a maximum of eighteen minutes.

The impact of overshare is that it can devalue everything that you say. People may stop listening or, depending on the content, feel too uncomfortable to listen to you.

You don't want to be known as someone to avoid or not listen to – that completely defeats the purpose. It's best to keep to the topic, stay focused on the key points, and present only information that is necessary and valuable for the audience.

Summary

Conciseness is a crucial aspect of communication. The smartest people are those who can present difficult things in an easy-to-understand way. Articulating your complicated concepts succinctly shows you as someone who has credibility and knows their stuff.

Our modern brains have lower attention spans now than ever before, and to capture people's attention, you need to do it instantly as you won't be able to hold it for too long. As is well known in the world of TED Talks, short and sharp is best.

It is important to follow the key principles of being concise:

- Clarity
- Key points
- The right words
- Brevity
- The final edit

This chapter also looked at what not to do – the dangers of oversharing. Sharing too much can ruin your reputation and devalue what you're saying.

FOUR
The Method

Now that you understand the need to be concise, you should think about the ideal means for delivering your message. It's likely you've all been in situations such as meetings or long phone calls, where you thought, *Man, that could have been an email.* You might also have received news in a text message that should have been explained on a phone call – hey, no one wants to get dumped by text.

This chapter will get you to think about the outcome you want from your communication. It's a critical question – once you understand your audience and the topic you're talking about, you'll want to share it in a sharp way, but what's the *point* of your communication? Understanding this will help you to determine the best way to deliver it.

This chapter will also look at a neat way to structure your written communications crisply, ensuring you provide the information someone needs and an outcome they can use. It's super-powerful stuff.

Your method for concisely presenting your message and value is important and I want you to get it right. Read on, and let's do it!

Determining the required outcome

Communication is one of the most powerful tools we have as humans. It's the cornerstone for interaction – the exchange of information, ideas and emotions. In the workplace, essentially everything we do is a form of communication. Whether it's Gina whipping up a report on sales for the month, Caitlin preparing a slide deck to train management in health and safety, or Kevin talking loudly about himself in the kitchen, there is ultimately always an outcome. It's important to think about the outcome you wish to have, as that will assist in deciding on the means to deliver the message.

Effective communication does more than simply transmit information from one person to another – it also establishes a connection and creates a new level of understanding. Successful outcomes often result because of clear and concise communication taking charge. Ultimately, being concise minimises misunderstanding and wasting that sweet, precious time we never have enough of. Thinking about the overall outcome you want as a result of the communication will affect:

- The format you use to present the message (if you get a choice)
- The techniques you use to share the information

Let's look at some of the outcomes you may want to achieve from your written and verbal communication.

Information sharing

One of the primary outcomes we would want from any communication is the dissemination of information. When you communicate, that information is then acquired by your audience and will hopefully be used for something important. In any event, once the information is shared, it's with someone else now to use. Your desired outcome is likely then for them to take action based on your communication.

Emotion and empathy

Thinking beyond just work, we use communication in all aspects of our worlds to share how we feel, and our words can evoke all types of emotions. If we use our communication right, we can connect on different levels with those around us. We get into the concept of connection later in the book, so stay tuned. For now: if we demonstrate empathy, those who are sharing their feelings can feel seen, which can lead to an enhanced social bond – a great outcome.

Influence

An important outcome we often aim for with our communication is the ability to be influential. For example, if I'm whipping up some legal advice, I generally want it to influence good decision making, and for my audience to do things that aren't illegal. If your communication is a marketing campaign, you want to influence people's buying habits. Whatever the type of communication, the power of your words can influence, and you want to be clear on the influence you're trying to achieve.

Inspiration and motivation

When we think of people in leadership roles, we regularly picture someone standing in front of a crowd and sharing a powerful message to motivate and inspire their teams. CEOs, teachers and professional speakers use their words to ignite fire, drive and passion from others. If the required outcome is to inspire action and amp up your people, a speech can be the most effective method. This is why conferences often have an inspirational speaker as their closing keynote, so people leave feeling excited, pumped and fuzzy.

Feedback

In the workplace, feedback is an important communication method and outcome. In an episode of my *Craft Messages That Matter* podcast (episode 6 – season 1 – Having difficult conversations with empathy in mind), I discuss how empathy plays a huge role in a feedback conversation, and that dishing out the classic 'shit sandwich' method is no longer appropriate. Specific methods of how to provide feedback would fill a whole book, but in short: the overall outcome should be to genuinely help the person receiving the information rather than hurting them. I think we've all suffered conversations that are more insulting than beneficial, where the information being thrown at us is only critical and not useful. If you are providing feedback, the overall outcome should be that the other person is better able to perform after the discussion, with clear actions to help them do so.

The outcome you're aiming for, as well as what value it can provide back to your audience, should be top of mind as you jump into preparing any communication.

Knowing the outcome can also help determine:

- The best method for sharing your communication
- How you structure your message
- How to clearly hit the message in the most effective way

What? So what? Now what?

The way you communicate and structure your messages can make a significant difference in how they are received by others. Sometimes, you don't need the formality and you can simply just shout the answer. In other circumstances, it can help to follow a structure so you can fully present the knowledge and solutions in a useable format.

Early on in my career, I discovered *What? So what? Now what?* – a transformative method that can be applied to both written and verbal communication. It provides a solid structure that allows you to position information well, and it puts your mindset in the right frame. Matt Abrahams from the Stanford Graduate School of Business explains that 'Communication structures serve as scaffolding for our messages. They allow us easy starting points, transitions, and clear endings.' Awesome, right?

The following structure has generally been used to apply a reflective activity amongst a group, when reviewing how an event or specific situation went down. It also works well as a framework for explaining a concept or idea, or for giving advice.

What?

Here you need to determine the critical bit of information that needs to be conveyed, to maximise the effects of your communication.

The What? stage is your opportunity to provide the context and to highlight the main point you will be answering or discussing. It's where you can clarify and outline that point, idea or question, as a means of leading the discussion. If your communication is in response to a request for information, the What? stage will help you demonstrate that you were listening to what you were asked, and it may also narrow down to the main point the other person is seeking help on.

So what?

This is where you will dig into the explanation part. It's where you:

- Explain your opinion
- Connect the question with the answer to support your audience
- Present your arguments

It's critical to remember to focus less on what you want to say and more on what your audience needs to hear. The ultimate question for this section is *What is the bottom line for my audience?*

This is where you provide your most valuable information and demonstrate your knowledge, highlight the key points and provide additional context to support what you're saying.

Now what?

This part focuses on the actions you want your audience to take as a result of what you have communicated. You need to highlight your main points, conclude on what you were saying, and add any next steps or calls to action. Include anything you need your audience to do, as a result of what you stated in the So what? section.

I'm a huge fan of this structure as it provides a logical flow for the information as well as the process for how you think. Noting the principle of conciseness, this technique also allows you to focus in on the information you want to share in the delivery, with sharp, useful information.

Imagine if everyone spoke and presented information in a logical and concise manner – messages would be clear, useful and effective. There are other ways we can concisely present information, including through the TEDx format, which we'll consider next.

The TEDx format and why it works

There are a few names that may pop to mind when you think of a TED Talk, which likely include Brené Brown, Simon Sinek and Sir Ken Robinson. These people have presented at TED or TEDx events, and their videos have sparked fandom for them and for their works.

TEDx is very close to my heart. As I mentioned in the introduction to this book, I'm the organiser of TEDxHobart and, at the time of writing, have pulled off two events. I've also presented my own TEDx Talk, titled *Lessons from my ethnic lunchbox.* You can say I know a thing or two about what makes TED and TEDx work. In case you don't know too much about TED:

- TED Conferences is the global phenomenon where ideas are shared with the world through a big conference held annually in Toronto. The polished and edited videos of those TED Talks then make it onto YouTube for the world to see.
- TEDx events are the locally organised mini versions of a TED conference, licensed under a city name or university. These TEDx events follow rules of curation and branding so there is consistency with the main TED Conferences event.

One of the things that make this franchise so fun is how short and sharp the presentations are, with each talk not meant to exceed eighteen minutes. While some people might think that's quite long for a presentation, eighteen minutes is considered bite-sized compared with most conference or academic presentations.

Short and punchy presentations that are structured in a particular way are incredibly effective. They deliver the key message and point – in the TED world that's called a *throughline* – together with interesting stories and anecdotes to ensure that people connect with and can remember the talk.

The whole mission of TED is to discover and share ideas that spark conversation, deepen understanding and drive meaningful change, so this particular format isn't for everyone and everything. When we talk about an 'idea', it is more than just a topic. A topic at an ordinary conference or event could be 'Why having a cat is a good idea', whereas a TED idea could be 'Why having a domestic cat as a pet can cure loneliness'. TED takes a topic and turns it into something more substantive.

In the spirit of conciseness, TED Talks are able to share often incredibly complex ideas and information in pocket-sized presentations. Years of work, research and experience are compiled into these digestible pieces of information, and TED Talks can have a reach of millions. This is the power of knowing how to package your knowledge and information concisely – you show your expertise and knowledge and demonstrate more credibility if you can present something complex in a clear and easy-to-understand format.

Would TED and TEDx events be the right method for you? It's an excellent platform, but it may not be right for the message you want to send. Regardless, you can still learn a lot from the TED way of delivering and from the presenters' ability to sharply deliver a complex message in a simple format. It's a challenge that takes some people months to perfect, but it is possible.

The power of PowerPoint

PowerPoint often gets a bad name, which is understandable. I know I'm not the only one who's sat through a terrible presentation feeling like my insides were being extracted each time a new slide appeared, and feeling dread when I saw we were only up to slide 6 of 78. However, when used well, PowerPoint can be an incredible tool for concisely communicating your message. If used in its appropriate manner, as a supporting tool to guide your talk, to direct your audience to think about things visually and to capture their attention, it can be the method you need.

TEDx Talks presenters rarely use slides, and there is a TED directive, 'Only use slides where it's necessary to explain your point'. I agree with this, but I want to provide an alternative perspective. When used well, slides can enhance your message and the audience experience.

Our brain can only do one thing at a time, so it doesn't like to read and listen at the same time. If you use slides that are filled with text and a heap of bullshit no one cares about, you'll lose people who may read through the content rather than listening to anything you're saying. It's better to use your slides to support the points you're making and give people a visual reminder for when they reflect on your points later. I'm a fan of using pictures – lots of them – to articulate points or to visually explain something I'm talking about.

I love this point raised by Jamie Cartwright on HubSpot:

> 'I like to think of Microsoft PowerPoint as a test of basic professional skills. To create a passing presentation, I need to demonstrate design skills, technical literacy, and a sense of personal style. If the presentation has a problem (like an unintended font, a broken link, or unreadable text), then I've probably failed the test. Even if my spoken presentation is well rehearsed, a bad visual experience can ruin it for the audience.'

Use words sparingly in your deck. You can use text, of course, but keep it light – short sentences, dot points, short quotes as an absolute maximum – or else you'll be competing with your slides for attention. If you're like me and you love attention, then you don't want a bundle of text to take everyone's gaze off you.

Let's not ruin things for the audience, yeah? This is your chance to dazzle with your wit, your words and your slides.

Choosing your communication means

Deciding on the most appropriate mechanism to share your message and to communicate will depend on a few different factors. Sometimes you won't have a choice – you will need to get up and speak in front of others (even if you are dying at the thought). Other times you can choose another option because, let's face it, you're the one who's doing the communicating. You might think an email is the easiest way to share the information you need to with accompanying documents, or perhaps sharing a short audio message is a quicker way to show your tone and get the message to someone. You just need to think of the most effective and concise way to get the point across.

In my corporate experience, I've had the joy of running training programmes to teach teams about things they'll need to know from a compliance perspective. If I force people together, I try and make it a fun time.

CASE STUDY: Alternative approach needed

When I worked for a larger legal team, we'd need to train different departments on areas of the law that would affect the practices. A senior colleague asked me to do a heap of research on a new privacy regime. I provided her with my findings, and she asked me to join her in running training for our marketing department. When the day arrived, what I thought was going to be a joint presentation turned into me sitting there watching her present. She got up with a bundle of notes in her hands and flicked through the different slides. All the work I had prepared was copied and pasted into at least fifteen different slides – all black text on a white background in Times New Roman font, and she read word for word what was included on each slide.

I glanced around the room and could see the pain in everyone's eyes. 'Did that guy fall into a coma?' said the person next to me, and to be honest, I was close to calling an ambulance. The presentation was long, boring and cringy.

At last, I had the opportunity to contribute something – an infographic – to this presentation. I stood up and said, 'I know this was a lot to take in, so as a way of having quick access to this information, I've whipped up a one-page infographic you can stick on your office walls and refer to when you need.'

Someone then raised their hands and said, 'Wouldn't it have made more sense for us to simply get that doc than to have sat through an hour of someone reading to me?'

Ouch, but they raised a valid point.

I could go on for ages about why this presentation didn't work, but for this context: perhaps a presentation simply wasn't the right way of communicating. Given the complex nature of the information, a long-winded presentation was most definitely a tiresome and exhaustive journey for everyone involved.

Knowing the best method to communicate a message and for it to remain effective is really important. Just because it's always been done a certain way doesn't mean that is the best way to do it every time. For the example above – providing training on a tricky and new issue – a shorter and more dynamic presentation could have been useful. I'd probably prefer a series of short training videos explaining the key concepts and why they're relevant for me, and some written resources to look at and refer to later.

Concisely providing a message in the most appropriate format will provide your audience with the value they're asking for and position you as the expert in the space.

Summary

Knowing the right method to communicate your message concisely can be a challenge. It's critical you understand the outcome you need from the communication to know the most appropriate way to share the message. When wanting to share a message to influence people's thoughts or actions, the written word or a presentation may be the most effective tools.

The What? So What? Now What? method gives us the scaffolding we need to position the information in a clear and easy-to-understand format. When we speak, we can think about the TEDx approach of breaking down a complicated concept into an accessible and short presentation.

Of course, presentations can benefit from a good set of PowerPoint slides. This method can be incredibly effective for sharing your messages if used well, with strong imagery and few words. Bad PowerPoints can be painful, long and boring, and presentations may not be the best way to communicate complicated and tricky information.

The idea of being concise, coupled up with the appropriate method of sharing, is vital when considering how you will deliver your message to your audience.

PART THREE
CONFIDENCE

Being confident in how you communicate means others will listen. This is a vital goal and will mean you can command the attention you deserve. Your voice will have authority and you'll smash it when you need to.

This part will go through your ability to sound confident in your voice and through the knowledge bombs you'll be dropping. It's a deep dive into how you can transform your communication to ensure that you present as confident and feel the courage in yourself to make it happen.

These two chapters will build you up to give you the courage to do the difficult things. You've got this.

FIVE
The Voice Of Confidence

Confidence is something a lot of us aren't born with. It's not something that suddenly dawns on us one day, and we say, 'I'm confident now!' It's one of those tools that builds over time.

No one is born as a naturally confident communicator – it's something we need to develop and continue through practice and experience. Even the best presenters feel some level of anxiety before a talk. The techniques we explore in this chapter will allow you to be the voice of confidence in those times where you feel you may not have it in you.

The chapter starts off by exploring the importance of truly believing in the message you're going to deliver. You'll then learn some techniques, which you can practise and play around with, to ensure that you don't let yourself down.

This chapter will get you thinking and help you tweak what you're doing to show your best and most confident self in just about any situation.

Feel the fear and believe in your message

Picture this: you're standing at the head of the boardroom table. You've been asked to present the results from a campaign you were running, and this is the first time the board of directors will hear about how it went. You are so petrified to be there; you're shaking and can't focus on the notes in front of you. These people are important. These people might be judging your work and may want to interrogate you.

Gulp.

So, what do you do? Being afraid to speak publicly is common. I've felt this terror and regularly do still feel a bit of fear anytime I go to stand up in front of a room. It's completely normal, though, and there is a reason we feel this fear.

To provide some context: the fear we feel comes from our evolutionary pasts. Evolution has made us very aware of our status amongst others. In the caveman era, we would hang out in groups of 100 or so people, and those with the highest status had better chances of survival with better food. They had the opportunity to find shelter and better chances of reproducing (if ya get what I mean). Their lives were on the line.

When there is any risk to our status, those good things we want and need are at risk. When we open our mouths and want to speak publicly, we fear we may lose our status by saying something silly and become a laughingstock. All this makes our bodies feel terror of public speaking. We feel a similar fear in other communication challenges such as providing constructive feedback or answering questions that are sprung on us, and we may use weak language when writing an email.

If you don't appear confident when you communicate, it may jeopardise your ability to influence with your message – you won't be making the impact you know you can and should make. When you're standing in that boardroom, you know you've done the work, and the results should be something you are proud of. It's only the thoughts swirling around in your head that are freaking you out.

You need to change that mindset. It's important to be able to move away from what others may think about you, as that will free up the concerns you hold and allow you to feel comfortable in what you're saying.

A tip for this is to shift the focus from what others may think of you and instead focus on the particular message you want to share and the impact it can make. This can empower you to feel confident in moving an audience to action rather than worrying about what they may think. The technique can be applied to all forms of communication.

The impact can have a ripple effect. That could be because you've presented the campaign results to the board, and now they think you're awesome. Or maybe you wrote an incredible email and, rather than being afraid that you'll cause a ruckus, you'll instead make change happen. Shifting the focus from you to the impact you can have removes the preconceived idea that you must be word-perfect and that everyone is judging you. Instead, the audience is there to listen and take in what you have to say. You'll sound confident, and you will be accepted as the person who knows the shit you're speaking about.

This might take some practice, but when it plays out, it can have an incredible effect.

TEDx preparation

As a TEDx organiser, I have the joy of making phone calls to our selected speakers and performers. It's one of my favourite parts of the whole process (and organising a TEDx event is a long process, to say the least).

CASE STUDY: TEDx speaker from my world

I once had a Zoom call with a speaker, who was one of the highest rated by our selection panel – the idea was exciting, we loved the speaker's story, and the alignment with our theme was perfect. The speaker had just about everything nailed. The only problem? They had little public speaking experience.

We knew that this person was doing some incredible work and that they'd be able to piece their idea together perfectly for the TEDx stage, yet they lacked the confidence to do it.

When I announced on the Zoom call that they would be speaking at TEDx, they looked at me with a blank face. I added, 'Is there a connection issue? I said you're going to be presenting at TEDx!'

They responded with 'Yeah, I can hear you...'

It was almost as if they were in shock and weren't sure how to respond. The person felt fear and a level of imposter syndrome. They had reasons to feel afraid and intimidated, including that their first language wasn't English, which made the prospect of doing their first ever presentation for up to eighteen minutes, unscripted, particularly scary. The mood didn't change much throughout the call – the person had seemed confused, as if we had made a mistake, and they clearly lacked confidence.

I knew that there would be work to do with this speaker but that it would ultimately work out.

Some weeks later, I ran a training session with our speakers on some communication techniques and things to think about in terms of crafting and delivering their messages. Part of this training includes the need to shift the focus away from themselves to thinking about the audience and the impact of their message. This is especially important with TED Talks, as the whole concept is about the idea itself rather than the individual.

The speaker came up to me at the end of the training and said 'I'm going to use this. You've helped me to understand it's less about me and really about how I can serve the audience with my message and the impact that I can make by standing on stage!' The shift and the focus happened.

On the day, the speaker stood on the red carpet and shared their story and idea. They told the story of the difficulty and adversity they faced, the challenges life threw at them, and the idea they established as a result. It was inspiring, heart-warming and powerful. Even though I'd heard the talk several times during rehearsals, it really hit me, and a few tears were shed (which I hate to admit).

Knowing the impact and the power a message can have should be more motivation to do your best than worrying about being word-perfect and hitting every point flawlessly. It takes practice to change your perceptions, but the shift can make a world of difference.

Make your voice sound confident

We've all been in those meetings where someone sounds really confident in what they're saying. They're loud, they use their hands, and they think they're the world's oracle. Yes, it is of course Kevin (or someone like him). Kevin believes he knows everything about stocks, cryptocurrency, socio-economic analysis and whatever else he decides to start talking about, because he is soooooo smart. Whether he actually knows anything about what he's talking about (a lot of the time, that is questionable) he *sounds* like he knows what he's talking about.

The difference between you and Kevin is that you'll actually know what you're talking about and be able to sound like you know what you're saying too. Sounding confident isn't only about speaking loudly, of course – it encapsulates:

- Developing the ability to command attention
- Applying principles of clarity and conciseness to present a crisp and clear message
- Using the right tone to share the message

This part of the chapter focuses on your voice when you speak and present. Some aspects can be applied to written communication as well. The following points explore things that can help.

Voice modulation

Varying the pitch and tone of your voice can add a new level of energy and enthusiasm, and an increased level of attention from those listening. A monotone has the potential to convey insecurity, or at the very least, will make it challenging to maintain the attention of your audience.

Following on from varying pitch and tone is your volume. Speaking softly has the potential to make others feel that you're uncertain. You need to find the right volume for the context to ensure you're allowing everyone to hear you and understand you. You can do this through emphasising key points in your talk, and when you practise, grab a pen and underline key words that you want to emphasise, so you know to stress the term more. You can also match your tone to the particular message you're sharing – if it's light-hearted and fun, you want to sound joyful and fun.

Articulation and pronunciation

Clearly articulating your words will make them clearer and prevent any misunderstanding, and careful enunciation will give everyone listening more comfort in what you're saying. Classic tongue twisters are an awesome way to improve your articulation. One I use from my drama class days is *Unique New York, New York unique*, repeating that and increasing in speed as you go.

Ensuring you pronounce words correctly is also important for improving your confidence. If you're sharing information that includes tricky words, practise them in advance. We all make mistakes, and that's fine, but preparation is the best way to prevent little accidents, which will make you feel and sound more confident.

Pace and pauses

It's important to be aware of how you come across, and your pace is a critical part of this. Speaking too fast sounds rushed and scared, while too slow can be frustrating for the audience. The average person speaks at 120–150 words per minute, according to Dom Barnard in VirtualSpeech. If you haven't figured out how many words per minute you speak, I'd love to recommend the tool Yoodli – an artificial intelligence speech coaching service platform that can:

- Record and transcribe your talks
- Identify any non-inclusive language
- Determine your pace and speed
- Calculate how many words per minute you speak

Yoodli is pretty cool and (at the time of writing) free. The rate you deliver your presentation should generally be a little slower than your average speaking rate, at a pace that sounds comfortable to ensure that the message is captured and lands with the audience. Your speaking rate when you present can impact how your audience perceives you – too fast? Maybe you're nervous. A steady pace will allow your audience to understand what you're sharing.

Another brilliant technique is implementing pauses. It's always essential to understand the context in which you're speaking to know how appropriate strategic pauses will be. If you're about to make a big point, perhaps something with shock factor, you may want to provide a pause first to build the anticipation. If you're sharing a story and before a big moment, you may want to create the dramatic effect and pause before continuing with the next aspect of the tale. A pause can be particularly effective just before you drop a knowledge bomb – *kapow*!

Body language and gestures

Closed-off body language gives the impression you're not feeling relaxed or comfortable. For example, standing with your arms crossed presents as someone who doesn't really want to engage and is blocking themselves from connecting with others. Conversely, having your arms free and gesticulating can help complement what you're saying. This is particularly true when you use your hands between your collar bone and navel – the 'influence zone' – showing that you're comfortable in sharing information.

These skills and techniques combined will help you to ensure that your message can be shared confidently. Never let your knowledge become secondary to your delivery. I want you to be able to walk into a room, share your value and be recognised for it. As you read on, you'll be able to add even more tools to your toolkit to enhance your voice of confidence. Kevin will never get to overshadow you again.

Change your words

We can sometimes sound less capable and less sure of ourselves simply because of the words we use or how our sentences are constructed. This is super-relevant to written communication and when you present in front of others.

To start with, there are a few words that can weaken your sentences and how others may view you. Those are 'think', 'just' and, in some contexts, 'but'. Words have the power to shape perceptions and can emphasise, diminish or even negate the point you're trying to make.

Saying 'I think'

Saying 'I think' demonstrates a level of uncertainty and doubt in what you're saying, potentially making others believe that you're not sure of yourself.

When I was a pharmacy assistant, someone asked me if a cream could be used to stop itching. I read the instructions and said, 'Well, I *think* it can be used for that.' The person then asked if there was someone else he could talk with. He didn't believe I knew what I was talking about, and fair enough too.

'I think' weakens the impact of what you're saying and can dilute the power behind any statement. Either removing 'I think' or replacing it with 'I believe' will strengthen what you're saying and help with the confidence you want to hold.

Including 'just'

'Just' is a common word and absolutely has its place in the English language. However, there are circumstances when it can diminish the impact of what you're looking to say.

Neuro linguistic programming (NLP) can help us understand how the way a message is conveyed can directly impact how anyone may receive it. NLP indicates that 'just' can send a message of subordination or apology, which may weaken your message and undermine your value (see The Coaching Room). For example, saying 'It's just that I thought it would make sense if…' creates a weaker message. You'd be better off simply saying 'It would make sense if…', ditching the fluff at the beginning.

'Just' also has the ability of making everything after it feel unimportant. Here's a little story to illustrate this: I was on the phone to a colleague several years ago, we were chatting away, and then he got interrupted by a builder working in the background.

'Hey sorry bud, I'm going to need to start drilling. Might be a bit loud!'

My colleague came back with, 'Yeah, that's fine! I'm just on the phone to our lawyer.'

Um – excuse me? You're *just* on the phone to your lawyer? Because I'm not important? It's fine to speak to me while there's drilling in the background? Come on…

I mean, I get it. I'm an internal person within the company, so a bit of banging and noise won't bother me. However, the use of 'just' implied I wasn't that important, devaluing me as a human.

Adding a 'but'

'But' is a useful word in everyday speech, yet it can also cause issues. A classic example is 'I'm not racist, but...' and you know the statement that will follow will almost always be racist. The term 'but' may negate what has come before it, and it can diminish the value of everything that comes after. 'But' can alienate others or piss you off when it's said to you.

Let's say your manager has asked you to make edits to a piece of work that required your expert opinion. You've gone to the effort to do the work and been thoughtful in your comments and mark-ups because you didn't want to rip the work apart. You then have a meeting with your manager, and she says, 'I appreciate the feedback you've provided on this, but...' It's at that point you get angry. You know that what's going to follow will simply diminish all the work that you put in. If this is what happens when you hear it, imagine how it could be interpreted by others you say it to.

Active voice

It's not only important to think about the words you use, but it's also critical to look at how you use them.

An active tone and voice will help you say things powerfully and clearly, without weak language ruining your influence. This is your opportunity to make your words more compelling and direct. A more passive approach isn't incorrect. It simply won't give you the best opportunity to be heard by those around you.

Here is a little example. You can say, 'The report was completed by me', which is passive; or you can say 'I completed the report', which is active. The active version has made it completely clear that you are in command and the one who did the work.

You don't want to muddy your message. The active voice gives you the chance to proudly state what you want to say without any confusion. It provides the voice of confidence you need to get your message across.

A few tweaks can improve how your voice comes across, particularly in the workplace. I want you to be able to confidently say what needs to be said and ensure that others don't think less of you because of a few inopportune words or careless sentence construction.

Calm yourself – box breathing

Sometimes, to appear and sound confident, we need to prepare ourselves to feel calm. Our breathing rate increases when we're feeling stressed, with shortness of breath often a symptom. A technique I love and teach my coaching clients and my TEDx speakers is box breathing.

A 2023 *Medical News Today* article explains, 'Box breathing is a powerful but simple relaxation technique that aims to return breathing to its normal rhythm after a stressful experience.... It may help clear the mind, relax the body, and improve focus.'

CASE STUDY: Box breathing in practice

I first discovered box breathing when I had a big public-speaking moment approaching. It was my twenty-third birthday, and I had to do a faculty moot – a simulated court proceeding – at law school. At the time, it was mandatory for everyone studying a Bachelor of Laws at my university to do their moot.

I had to show up to the court, in full suit and tie, and stand up in front of one of our lecturers and someone from the legal profession, both of whom were acting as judges. I'd done all the necessary studying, and this was one of the final stepping stones to passing the degree. I was nervous.

Before heading off to the courts, I was at home getting ready and feeling anxious. I wasn't sure how to calm down so did a quick Google search, discovered box breathing and gave it a try. After doing it a few times, I started to feel calmer.

I got a taxi to head over to the courts and continued box breathing in the car. I arrived at the courts feeling

> comfortable and prepared and was able to spend some time having a laugh with my friends before we presented.

Through research, I've learned that people with high-stress jobs will also often use box breathing when their bodies are in fight or flight mode. It allows us to recentre ourselves and improve our concentration.

How do we do box breathing? It's a simple, four-step process:

1. Breathe in for four seconds
2. Hold the breath for four seconds
3. Breathe out for four seconds
4. Hold the breath for four seconds

Note: breathe in through your nose and out through your mouth.

I like to repeat this a few times as it seems to help centre me. It's something you can do wherever you are. For best results, though, sit somewhere with your back supported in a comfortable chair, with your feet on the ground.

This is an easy technique to remember, and the image below is a great visual representation to help you keep the concept in mind.

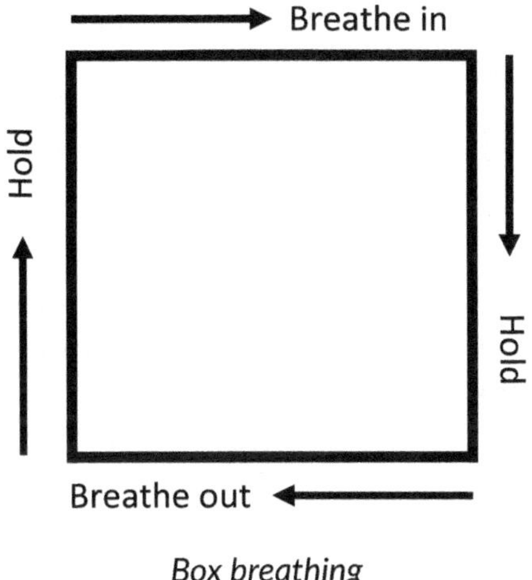

Box breathing

You always want to gain back control and ensure you're feeling as comfortable and confident as you can be. Ensuring you can control your physical self and your reactions will be critical for those moments when you need to present.

Nail the presentation preparation process

One way to be sure that you will be confident and comfortable to speak, particularly when delivering a presentation, is to follow a process when you are preparing. You feel less confident when you don't have control, and a process gives you the opportunity to gain control because you know what you need to do and how to do it. This process will also give you the mental confidence required to make sure you're ready and amped up to present your thoughts at work, at an event, or anywhere else. It's a process I always follow, and I know it's helped my one-on-one clients heaps as well. Let's do this!

1. Research and prepare

Knowing your subject matter inside and out will provide the level of confidence you need to cover off those feelings of imposter syndrome. You absolutely know what you're talking about, and doing additional research work can help resolve that in your mind.

2. Pick no more than three key points

As outlined in the presentation structure we covered in Chapter Two, it's important to keep with no more than three key points. This is more than enough for your audience to take in, and those points will become your structure. More than three, and you may overwhelm them (and their limited attention spans).

Think about the key outcome you want people to walk away with from listening to the presentation, and then determine the three key points which will make the desired outcome and actions clear for the audience.

3. Illustrate those three key points

Something we will dig into in Chapter Nine is the importance of appealing to everyone in the audience through how people like to understand information – that is, to hit both the left brain and right brain. Briefly: the best way to achieve this is to combine factual information, statistics and research studies (left brain); and support that with stories, videos and images (right brain). This provides a full spectrum of the key points, allowing each person in the audience to embrace what you've said. For example, some people will obsess over the statistics, while others will love the stories. Also, people will remember the facts and figures because they'll connect them with the story or image used to illustrate the point.

4. Create your materials

Now that the hard work is done, you may decide to whip up some materials to bring the presentation to life. It is always essential to know what you're saying first and then create your supporting materials later. Included in this category is your slide deck – yes, the classic PowerPoint!

The absolute worst thing you can do is think 'I need to do a presentation. I know, I'll open up PowerPoint and get cracking.'

No.

As discussed in Chapter Four, PowerPoint can provide an amazing visual aid to support your message and guide what you say, as you'll associate the slides with what you want to say. It also provides structure for when you're speaking: introduction, key point 1 with facts, figures, then stories and images and conclusion of point, then move on to key point 2, and so on up to the conclusion.

5. Practise

I'm sure I don't need to tell anyone how essential it is to practise before delivering a presentation. Practice leads to a better result because you've already done the presentation so you become more comfortable doing it. Practise everywhere and anywhere, and as often as you can.

Particularly when you're presenting at an event, you'll want to rely more on memory than on your notes, so becoming comfortable and regularly practising your talk will give you the confidence you want when it's showtime.

6. Record yourself

Recording yourself might feel uncomfortable at first, but it is one of the best techniques to improve your technique and understand what you're doing. It's important to record yourself both on audio and video, and then listen to and watch the recordings so you know how you come across. This allows you to be critical in assessing yourself and to pay attention to what you like or what you may not like and wish to improve. Here are some additional tips:

- First, listen only. You'll pick out things specifically without the distraction of watching yourself. Make notes as you listen back to your recordings.
- Watch yourself without the sound. The recording may be of your whole body or only your head, but this will help you understand what you do and notice any unusual things or tics you're normally not aware of. I find that I do weird things with my hands sometimes!
- Bring it all together. Watch and listen to the audio and visual recording, write down additional notes on your observations – things you like, things you want to improve, and things you want to stop doing.

Doing this for each presentation will guarantee you'll improve your skills. You'll also become aware of the things that may detract attention from your communication, allowing you to present in a way you're proud and excited about.

7. Go out there and do it!

With all of this preparation, you'll be feeling confident and ready to be the best version of yourself on stage. Step onto that stage (or into the boardroom, meeting room, Zoom room), breathe out, and speak, not forgetting to focus on the impact of your message rather than on yourself.

Having a process in place gives you the control and confidence you need with something that can otherwise be terrifying, especially if it's something you're not doing regularly.

Summary

The voice of confidence is far more than just speaking loudly and hoping for the best. You need to believe in what you're saying and feel confident in the message you're delivering. This chapter has given you a presentation preparation process that you can apply to any public speaking opportunity, giving you the control and confidence you need to smash a talk.

Breathing can assist us to feel comfortable and happy. Using the box breathing technique can assist you to feel comfortable and calm you down so you are ready to speak in any situation.

Sometimes the language you use can let you down and diminish the impact you're trying to make. Avoiding the use of 'I think', 'just' and 'but' can have a significant impact on your influence and how others perceive what you're saying. Ultimately, though, you need to believe in what you're saying. If you don't believe in the message you're sharing, and the impact it can make, you will struggle to be comfortable with what you're doing.

SIX

Knowing Your Abilities

Sometimes, that little voice in your head makes you think that you can't or shouldn't be the one to speak on that stage or present the report to the board because you don't know enough. There might be some circumstances where you might be a bit 'delulu' (delusional) in your abilities, yet a lot of the time, you are in fact the right person to be sharing on the particular matter at hand.

This chapter will go through the best ways in which you can establish your credibility, ensuring that you use the skills you've obtained in your career, in business or in education within a talk or written piece.

There is a major takeaway in this chapter: your education and experiences are valuable. As is stated in the book *Key Person of Influence* by Daniel Priestley, 'You are standing on a mountain of value.' Everything that you've learned and experienced in your life and work means that you have valuable and useful expertise, particularly when that education or experience relates to the matter you've been asked to speak on or write about.

Establishing your credibility

We're generally asked to speak on something or prepare a report when people know we're experienced in that area. That choice could be based on a number of factors that make you the right person to be sharing your message with an audience.

How do you know if you're the right person? Generally, you'll know if you have the credibility to share your knowledge on the topic at hand. We can all doubt ourselves, though, so I'll outline some factors to help determine whether you are in the best position to do the work.

Your unique value proposition

Think about what makes you the most appropriate person to be on that stage. If you're genuinely doubting yourself, it may be a sense of imposter syndrome – that voice whispering into your ears, making you think you're not the person who should do this. However, if you sat down and pulled out a piece of paper and went through the following list, you may realise that this opportunity and your knowledge are a perfect fit.

Education

There is a very strong likelihood, if you're reading this book, that you have a high level of education. Whether that education was through a training organisation, university, a college, whatever – you likely spent years to gain your qualifications. Through this, you have learned a lot and, as a result, have plenty of knowledge to impart. I know for me, having a Bachelor of Arts, Bachelor of Laws and a Graduate Diploma of Legal Practice provides me with authority to talk about a lot of things from a legal perspective. When I'm the only one who has those qualifications, I become the only person who is capable of speaking on these points. An example of this is one of the boards I've been part of. When a question of law pops up that the business needs to consider, I am the only person who can comment.

Experience

Beyond that of education, your experience is a huge reason – and I mean an absolutely enormous reason – why you'll probably be the authority to present on something.

CASE STUDY: A whole new approach

I got asked to speak at a conference in New Zealand because of something I did in my experience as a lawyer.

To provide some context: when I worked in a very large research and teaching business, the workflow process could be very slow. With most of the matters I worked on, I needed a lot of input from different aspects of the business to get the project off the ground.

For one project in particular, I needed to speak with the project manager, the lead researcher, the financial controller, the insurance brokers, the technology transfer officer, the compliance manager and the clinical trial officer. It was exhausting.

Ordinarily, someone would email everyone individually to seek advice, and this type of process could take months to complete. Instead, two other people and I came together and said, 'Let's change how we do this.' We brought everyone together for a kick-off meeting and walked through what would need to be done. We had our specific tasks included in an online project management system (this is very common now, but it was very advanced in 2017!) and held regular stand-up meetings to check in and ensure all was on track.
A process that used to take up to three to four months took us only three weeks – it was awesome.

I spoke about some of this great work and our new approach, after which I and the other administrative lead were asked to present on this experience in New Zealand. Our achievement was considered important and innovative, and the conference organisers wanted

> to hear all about it, which then also secured us a speaking slot at an international conference!
>
> My ability to describe this real-world experience and demonstrate the results it had on the business established that I had the authority to speak on this matter. I'm not a project management expert, yet I was called to give what was essentially a project management-focused talk. This presentation also then inspired some of my own talks and some of the keynotes I deliver on communication and collaboration.

This is how you can show that you are the right person to be speaking and presenting on a particular topic: you have the scars and the metaphorical battle wounds to show that you have done the work, have the knowledge and can get up there and show the world that you know this. If you don't have the full spectrum of knowledge you may need, you still have the opportunity to dig in a bit deeper and build that knowledge base.

It's important to do an assessment of or an audit on what you may not know so you can feel extra prepared for the opportunity to communicate on the matter. You don't need to know everything, but when you're aware of what you don't know, you can strive to fill those knowledge gaps and improve your level of understanding. This will help you grow and allow you to continue to be the authority you know you can be in your topic and interest area.

Your work, your education and your experience combined are what makes you the person who can speak and show your audience that you know your shit and can present it to the world at large. When you don't have some of this stuff, though, proving that you're the right person for the job can be more challenging.

CASE STUDY: 'Let me do it!'

For a lawyer and governance professional, being part of a range of professional memberships is standard practice. This usually gives you a few extra letters to add to your name, it gives you access to attend networking events, and it looks pretty good on the CV too. With one of my memberships, I joined the voluntary committee to run things locally in Tasmania, such as coordinating and organising our professional development and networking events, encouraging members to contribute to the association and help build the community, and also to get involved at the national level. The association used to run a magazine, too, which I was a big fan of. I'd written several articles over the years for the magazine, as this is a good thought-leadership development, and it always helps to put your name out there. Free publicity is good publicity, as they say.

As I was the divisional association leader in my state, I was building the brand and the community locally. One of our members was in a mixed legal and information governance role. They asked if they could write an article for us on a banking royal commission matter that was occurring in the public arena. When I asked a few questions about their experience in this area, it transpired they didn't have direct knowledge, only insights gathered from media sources.

At the same time, I'd heard from a barrister who had some involvement in this banking royal commission matter, and who wanted to share some interesting insights that in-house lawyers across Australia could consider as a result of what was happening. It made sense – this second person had first-hand experience and the information to make it relevant, and they knew how to communicate it for that particular audience.

Comparing the two authors, it's an obvious choice which one is the right person to share on this message. Doing the shit is sometimes one of the most important things you can do to build your credibility to be the right person to talk about something.

Doing the shit

If you've been asked to speak on something for a conference, there is a good chance you know a lot about the topic. When you do the shit, you get recognised for it and sought after to share your perspective on it. You may have established your credibility and created enough trust to be identified as the authority on the topic. If you've put your hand up to share on something, this is now your chance to show that you know about it.

Of course, one of the best ways to show people that you know what you're talking about is to demonstrate that you've actually done it. You may be the expert on privacy because you worked on a major compliance project, or maybe you know all about social media marketing and have increased engagement for a client by 250% – because you've done the work, you know about it.

Here are three ways you can show your audience that you are the authority:

1. **Experience**

   You've done the work, and you know the topic like the back of your hand. Being able to share your thought leadership through platforms such as LinkedIn or through word of mouth, because people know you're good at this, can be important. Having substantial knowledge in a particular space because you've been there, you've researched, you've got the runs on the board – this is the stuff that demonstrates to the world that you know this and are the right person to be speaking or writing on this matter.

2. **Being the expert**

   You don't need to be the world's expert in a particular area, but you should definitely know enough to say you have expert knowledge. It is never safe to hold yourself out as a leader on a topic if you haven't done the work to back it up. You need to develop that deep knowledge – through education, training or hands-on experience – and be able to say you know enough to be an expert. Every piece of work completed, article read, email sent or report written forms part of the research and work that allows you to call yourself an authority and build on the knowledge you've gained. This will not only help you when it comes to communicating that information out with the world; it will also instil further confidence in your audience as well.

3. **Demonstrating the results**

   If you've done the shit, had the experience and got the notches on your belt to prove it, you can show this in your presentations and written work. Use the data you've gathered and your case studies to present how much you know about the topic at hand, and you'll be able to show your authority in this space.

As well as convincing other people, having the experience and the expertise builds courage in your own abilities, reminding you that you know what you're talking about. You may sometimes have some self-doubt, but it's important to recognise your own knowledge and experience, giving yourself the confidence to claim that you are an authority in your area.

The TED approach to credibility

The TED and TEDx worlds bring together the right people to present on particular ideas they know about. Despite many people dreaming of pitching for the opportunity to stand on one of those red carpets and have their talk blasted across YouTube, there is one essential element that many of those dreamers do not have. That is a level of credibility.

Don't get me wrong, they may be brilliant and knowledgeable people, but they also need to have the experience, have done the work and have a name within the community around their sometimes very niche idea. TED Conferences don't reveal all of their secrets for curating speakers, but they do have a specific team that review and search through people who are recommended to them, conducting their own research based on what they've found in the media and by attending conferences and events. TEDx events are a little more relaxed, noting that they're the smaller, community-based events, yet they're still required to follow curatorial guidelines.

How TED and TEDx curators view credibility is based on factors, including:

1. **Social proof:** There is existing evidence of the work and the impact that a person's specific idea has had on the world, and they're doing

something specific that others are interested in. That social proof and evidence can support you in demonstrating that you know your shit and are the right person to be communicating about a topic.

2. **Expertise:** The person has expertise in the subject matter and can show this through a body of work. This may be work they've done in their role or through experience, which demonstrates why they're the person who should be speaking on this.

Let's check out three examples of TED or TEDx speakers who have been identified as having the relevant expertise to present on their topic.

1. Brené Brown

A stranger to no one who has the internet, Brené Brown is an American professor, author and podcast host. She has spent the past two decades researching and publishing on the topics of leadership, shame and vulnerability. This work provided her the opportunity to present at TEDxHouston in 2010, with *The power of vulnerability* becoming one of the most watched TEDx Talks ever. Brené's experience and knowledge, through her research, made her the most appropriate person to be speaking on that topic, and her communication extended after that talk into a range of books, TV series and research papers.

2. Tim Urban

Tim is the co-founder of the website Wait But Why, which is a long-form blog with illustrations. The blog produces a lot of content on many topics, including artificial intelligence, procrastination and outer space, to name a few. Some of the posts gained a lot of popularity, and the idea behind one of the posts became the subject for Tim's TED Talk, *Inside the Mind of a Master Procrastinator*. Tim was recognised as someone who had researched and knew this topic and was therefore identified as someone who was able to present on it.

3. Cameron Russell

Cameron is an American supermodel and now an activist. As a model, she has appeared at fashion shows for designers such as Chanel, Prada, Versace and Louis Vuitton. She was asked to speak on the TEDx stage for a talk titled *Looks aren't everything. Believe me, I'm a model.* This talk is based around her experience in having won the 'genetic lottery', following the societal standards of what is considered attractive. Her honest approach, and her acknowledgement of the privilege she has received on the basis of her appearance, demonstrated her lived experience and was truly mind-blowing for the audience.

The TED and TEDx stages provide excellent examples of how you can be credible as long as you have done the work.

Summary

When you've done the work, and you have the stories and scars to prove it, you're ready to share and speak on your area of expertise. Doing the shit and being the authority means that you've got the runs on the board. That little voice in your head should be pushed aside when you know you have gained the knowledge and experience, you've done the work, and you've earned the place to speak or write on a topic.

As we've seen from the TED and TEDx space, if you have the education, the experience and the personal brand to show that you are an expert in a particular space, you will also have the credibility to share your voice.

When you do the shit, you can be the authority to present on it. Don't let those voices in your head stop you.

PART FOUR
CREATIVITY

There are things you can do to spice up your written and verbal communication to change and improve how you spread your message, ensuring that it's right for the audience and in service of them.

When you inject some creativity in your communications, you will experience a whole new level of engagement.

Remember: your communication isn't only about getting a result for yourself. It's also about providing value to the people who need to hear it.

If you get those creative juices flowing, nothing can stop you.

SEVEN
Thinking Outside The Box

In the world of communication, implementing some difference is a godsend. Just like in other aspects of your life, a little bit of difference is a good thing.

Can you imagine if everyone walked around wearing beige jumpsuits all day? It would feel like a militant camp. Your communication is the same. If you did everything the same as all the other communication channels, you'd never be able to maintain people's attention.

Thinking outside the box and implementing creativity when you share information can capture attention and hold it in ways you weren't expecting. This chapter explores why the usual, standardised ways of communication can be on the boring side and considers ways you can inject some creativity.

There are so many awesome ways you can inject and integrate creativity into your communication methods, and I'll share some of my favourite ways and the tools you can use to make everything work.

Why the usual can be boring

Imagine this: you're tasked with giving a presentation to your team showing the end-of-quarter results. You've done plenty of work to improve your presentation and public speaking skills, and you are pumped to show the team the awesome work you and the team have achieved.

You absolutely want to smash this, because you know who's going to be in the room? Kevin. Bloody Kevin will be there, and he'll be annoying as ever, with his charismatic charm and ability to ask smart questions and sound confident.

You create an outline of what will be discussed; you grab the relevant information, statistics and some success stories from clients; and you have a plan regarding the key messages and information you're sharing.

You jump into Canva and create some dynamic slides with great visuals. You don't add too much text because you know that everyone will simply read the slides instead of listening to you. You're feeling good so far. You need to get approval from your boss for the slide deck, so you send it through. Her response: 'This isn't in the company PowerPoint template. There isn't enough information to know what's going on, and there are too many pictures. Start again.'

This would sting.

Ultimately, it would be painful for everyone in the room. If you're presenting information using the company-branded PowerPoint presentation, with a heap of text, in a generic font, it's going to feel a drag, and no one will engage with the content. This is the same when it comes to your written communications. If you're writing a report that is in size 12 font, Times New Roman and twenty-seven pages too many, it'll take people way too long to read and get stuck into.

Following the standard methods can simply become boring. Here are a few other points to think about:

1. **Not personal:** The conventional, same ol' way of communicating or presenting is often too generic. As I've raised before, considering who your audience is will make a big impact regarding how and what you communicate with them,

and the most appropriate method for doing so. Otherwise, it can be hard for the message and content to resonate with those who may really need it.

2. **Predictable:** It can be hard to captivate an audience when what they're seeing or reading looks identical to what they've been exposed to several times. When something feels predictable, it is a challenge to give it your full attention. We know that the next slide will have five dot points, someone might try and be funny and include a meme that was popular in 2012, and there will be a block of text to polish things off. *Yawn.*

3. **Boring:** Not everything needs to be fun and exciting, but it shouldn't feel like torture either. If a presentation feels like a lecture, or a fifty-page report feels like a slow and painful murder, no one is going to engage with the content.

Injecting creativity into the way we communicate can add new life and encourage active listening, attention and care. Consider this story, referenced in PwC Australia's 2017 report 'The Power of Visual Communication'. A citrus farming operation enlisted the help of a lawyer to create a pictorial contract using comic images to engage fruit pickers – fruit pickers were generally considered 'vulnerable employees with low levels of literacy'. The contract explained the complex concepts included in the agreement entirely visually, making it accessible to every recipient.

It's not every day you see a visually depicted contract, yet in these circumstances it was the perfect solution to bridge the communication gap, and it helped the particular audience understand the message. It's also likely that the fruit pickers would remember what the agreement contained more readily than others who may not have a clue what's included in their text-heavy, lawyer-speak employment agreement.

Research suggests that we are better at remembering content when we've seen it in picture form instead of text. This is known as the *picture superiority effect*, which was first identified in 1976 by Douglas Nelson, Valerie Reed and John R Walling. The reason this may be the case is that picture stimuli are embedded twice into our memory, as both verbal code and as an image. When you add visual elements into a presentation, the audience will have extra stimuli to embed and remember the message.

There is plenty of support to suggest that adding creative elements to written and verbal communication can play a massive part in its ability to engage and capture your audience to listen. In the corporate world, where everything is generally dull in colour, you can be a sparkling unicorn, sharing colour, stories and messages that resonate and capture the hearts and minds of those in the room.

You should always consider how you can best implement these creative elements. Let's take a dive into the world of marketing and some principles you should consider using.

AIDA – learning from marketers

I'm a big believer in learning a lot from different industries – techniques and experience from one industry can often be applied nicely to others. This time, we'll consider the world of marketing. Marketing is of course all about communicating a message to the wider world and using the power of conviction to sway an audience to do a certain thing. Often that thing is to buy something, or might be about persuading someone to do something such as to vote for one political candidate over another.

There is a classic marketing technique, AIDA, which can have an amazing application in the world of communication and public speaking. It excites me possibly more than it should.

AIDA is an acronym for attention, interest, desire, action. It was developed by American advertising and sales extraordinaire Elias St Elmo Lewis in the late nineteenth and early twentieth centuries, and it is still considered the cornerstone for modern marketing practices. Omitting just one of the four steps is likely to lead to an unsuccessful result. When each element of AIDA is applied in a communication context, a lot of value can be extracted.

1. Attention

This all about getting the attention of the audience you're communicating with. In the marketing world, for example, advertisements in unusual places grab people's attention.

In the communication world, you want to find things that have the same effect. For example, starting with a really strong opening such as a shocking statistic or a surprising story to get your audience interested and spark their curiosity to want to learn more.

2. Interest

Next you need to keep the audience's interest and hold it long enough for them to absorb the information you're sharing. As discussed earlier, using concise information and plain English is important, to ensure the audience won't be distracted by confusing words or concepts and instead will be keen to keep listening in.

As we considered with PowerPoint presentations, using powerful images and switching between images and text (not much text, mind you) can be helpful in capturing and maintaining the interest of the audience.

3. Desire (or decision)

In the marketing world, this part of AIDA is about highlighting a product's features and showing how it is superior – the value proposition – including the benefits that may entice someone to want to make a purchase.

This is exactly what you want to do with the concept, topic or idea you're communicating to your audience. It's about showing your perspective and being convincing. If you're looking for someone to listen to something important, this is where to include the meaty stuff to sell your message.

4. Action

This is the step where you want your audience to do something with the information you've provided. For example, in a work context, are you trying to make a business case for some software? At a conference, are you presenting on better ways for a business to manage its operations and telling everyone the methods to do so?

You want to ensure the perceived value will motivate the audience to do something with the information provided; otherwise, you're only sharing information for the sake of sharing.

Being creative in your communication is important, and learning from other industries can encourage different thinking and new ways of producing an outcome that can only be beneficial to you, particularly if you want to break through and get stuff to happen.

CASE STUDY: COVID creativity examples from the USA

In the world of beige, sometimes being purple is a good thing. When the messaging and communications are all the same, they get boring and no one cares about what's going on. When a presentation is someone standing behind a lectern with vanilla slides, speaking in a monotone voice, you may find yourself wanting to stab yourself in the eye with your pen instead of using it to write any notes down! (Please don't stab yourself in the eye, though.)

In a bid to be purple, ie grab attention and get the message across, the US government engaged creative agency WORK Labs to generate targeted advertising in a time when it was important to get the message heard.

Here are a few examples from the campaign, as shown by Muse.World:

- Act like you have an ankle monitor on. Stay home.
- Act like 90% of belly buttons. Stay in.
- Act like your ex just walked into the party. Practice social distance.

These ads were displayed on bright backgrounds and shared digitally, ideal for the audience they were targeting. Through the power of creativity, these images and text influenced people's decisions. Reflecting the AIDA technique above:

1. The colours of the campaign caught the attention of the audience.
2. The text was concise and funny, keeping people's interest.
3. The information was relatable and therefore desirable.
4. There was a clear call to action in each final sentence.

Using a bit of humour and, most importantly, creativity when speaking to people can help break through the rubbish and make your message a more memorable and powerful experience.

You don't need to always do things the same way – you can do things differently for the benefit of the audience and to get your message to hit the mark. Diversifying your approach to both your written and verbal communications not only sparks interest, but it will also make sure your message resonates with your audience. You can open the doors to innovation and find new ways to capture attention.

Creative communications

There are so many awesome ways you can communicate information to people and ways you can integrate technology to be more effective. In a corporate environment, there are always things you can inject to add some colour, fun and creativity to a plain-Jane, standard piece of communication to make it work for your audience.

I'll share a few creative communication methods and explain how they can be used for written communication at work, plus some techniques and tools for presentations. A lot of these are things I've tested myself or regularly use.

1. Infographics

Sometimes, having all your information typed out in a formal letter style is boring. It might be well written, but it doesn't jump out and make you want you to read it. Using infographics to present your information forces you to focus on key messages and main points, and it encourages you to use concise information to present the information. Not sure what an infographic is? Terrell Hanna of TechTarget defines it, 'An infographic (information graphic) is a representation of information in a graphic format designed to make the data easily understandable at a glance.'

Infographics are particularly useful to simplify your communications and share key information in a visually appealing manner. If you're wondering how you can make one, I've found that the online tool Canva is an easy (and free) platform to whip up an infographic and edit it, adding a number of visual elements to show what you're saying.

2. Videos

Recording a video is sometimes the most effective method of communication. Instead of writing an email or a message, it can be way simpler to grab your phone, set it up facing you, and record a little video. Rather than sending endless work emails that'll get lost in the rubble, shoot a short video across, and it will get noticed.

In presentations, including video clips can help break up the (potential) monotony of someone talking. If you can't find a video that illustrates what you want to share, create one yourself! A tool I've used previously, Powtoon, is a video maker where you can create cartoons of stories and characters with their animation tools. It can be a bit of fun, so why not give it a try?

Where you know there is a video that illustrates the point you're making, chucking it into your presentation can be captivating. I've used TikTok videos, YouTube clips and all sorts of other things from online to help show what I'm talking about.

3. Asynchronous communication using Loom

On the video creation train, you can completely transform the way you connect and share information in the workplace with asynchronous forms of communication, ie where people are communicating at different times. Emails are a basic example – you send an email, and the recipient replies later.

Technology such as Loom allows you to create content from your screen, featuring yourself as well with video and audio, which you can then share later with your audience. Loom allows you to add text comments and replies at time-stamped sections, so all conversations remain in the one platform. This can be an easier way of communicating an idea or concept to someone, and a creative way to share information that doesn't require you to be there to answer questions. Seems handy to me.

4. Voice notes

Sometimes sharing your message in an audio format is more effective than written communication. Voice notes are a nice way of personalising how you communicate, as the person can hear your tone and understand your emotions, which provides a more human element to what you're saying. For example, people sometimes connect with me on LinkedIn and share a voice note to say hello rather than an impersonal written message. At work, for something you want to get across quickly, rather than sending an email, you could send a voice note outlining the highlights and then follow it up with the detailed email to cover yourself for later (you can tell I'm a lawyer when I say things like this!).

If you use Gmail, you can download a Chrome extension called Vocal, which allows you to record and attach audio files to your emails. Otherwise, there are messaging apps like Slack, WhatsApp or Signal that allow you to shoot off a voice note instead of text messages. Anna Codrea-Rado wrote an article for *Business Insider*, describing how she experimented sending voice notes instead of email in her consultancy. She soon started landing better-paying work and now also uses messaging tools to communicate with friends. I did like this quote from her article: 'Adding in some audio made my otherwise cold inbox thaw a little.'

5. Gamification and interactive elements

Sometimes, all you need is an interactive activity to get the audience to participate and to ensure they're listening. Gamification – adding game-like elements to any task – is particularly useful in training programmes, where you can throw a reward at someone for getting a correct answer or for simply participating at all.

Tools such as Kahoot! or Slido can allow you to ask a question of the audience and gather a range of information back from them. This can lead to real-time conversations with the audience to understand their thoughts and perspectives on the issues at hand.

6. Simplifying those slides

I won't bang on about this too much as I've covered it in detail in Chapter Four, but having impactful slides in your PowerPoint presentation will amplify your presentation significantly. Moving away from blocks of text to images, videos and colour will allow the audience to listen to you, with your slides acting as a reference tool.

The saying *Show, don't tell* comes to mind. Using PowerPoint as a reference tool to help you explain and convey the message is far more useful than relying on it to say the message for you. Once you have mapped out and planned everything you want to say, the next step is to create a creative slide deck with strong visuals and videos, to convey the message in a dynamic way rather than assaulting an audience with buckets of text.

CASE STUDY: Making a business out of creativity

I'd like to tell you about my friend Sarah who lives in the UK. Sarah and I first connected when I saw a meme she'd shared on Instagram. I responded to her post, and we engaged in a conversation. We learned that we were both in-house lawyers who were trying to do things differently.

Sarah would make TikTok and Reels clips, talking about the pains in-house lawyers face in their roles. A favourite of mine was an image of a haunted house with the text 'Accept liquidated damages or sleep in a haunted house?' Then we see Sarah carrying a pillow and running towards the entrance of the house. Hilarious!

There were a few things Sarah used to grab people's attention, but a lot came down to the creative ways she would communicate in relatable and fun ways. One post in particular was an infographic titled 'What You Think You Can Do With a Law Degree vs The Reality'. It had a picture of an iceberg, with the attractive, conventional legal jobs on the iceberg above the surface, while under the water was the range of other, vaguely law degree-related jobs. This post exploded – it received thousands of views, comments and likes from people across the globe. Sarah then continued using these creative means of communication to share relevant and relatable information. She was building an audience and realised that her content-sharing skills were unique, enabling her to cut through the noise that existed online.

After a change of jobs, from in-house lawyer to commercial director of a legal tech company, Sarah took the leap to work for herself with her business, Law But How? It started as her side hustle but soon expanded into her full-time job. Her business assists legal professionals in increasing their visibility and creating opportunities for themselves on social platforms through visually appealing content. Sarah implements many of the tips and tricks that we consider in this book, but ultimately, she teaches lawyers how they can communicate effectively and creatively with potential clients and the wider world through social content.

Summary

Using creativity to communicate a message can vastly improve the way in which it reaches and engages with your audience. Thinking outside of the box when it comes to delivery can help ensure that your message lands effectively and hits the mark. If you give people what they've always received or expect to receive, the chances of them caring are low. Using some of the fun tools available when you speak or write can dramatically impact how information is interpreted and received.

This chapter explored the advertising principle of AIDA to consider how you should consider positioning your communications to make them as effective as possible. We also explored some of the awesome tools and techniques available for use when presenting, public speaking or creating a written piece of work, and how this can transform what you're saying and create a new level of connection.

EIGHT

Making The Standard Stuff Fun

If you're working for a big corporation, there may be some strict guidelines you'll be required to follow for any internal or external communication. This is totally understandable because there can be risks associated with 'work stuff' in writing, and anyone could be watching at a conference. However, you should never let the risk factor or fear factors prevent you from adding in some creative elements to make the communication engaging.

This chapter explores how you can make the ordinary forms of communicating that little bit better. I provide some practical examples you can use right now to turn an email into something appealing rather than it being a big block of text, or to throw in some interaction and make a presentation come to life.

Making the usual better

Your company may be strict with the use of PowerPoint, forcing you to use a regimented company slide deck. They might not let you create infographics to share complex information, implement audience participation software for your presentations, or create TikToks or short videos as a way of sharing information. I get it – it's annoying.

However, if you are stuck with the same old means of sharing information, you can still introduce elements of creativity to create that spark your audiences want, and what you need to have your voice and value heard. As we know, creativity plays a vital role in capturing your audience's attention. Don't underestimate the power of emotion and how important it is to connect with your audience (Serhat Pala).

I have a few tricks up the ol' sleeves that will be useful in adding some creativity into how you present and communicate.

1. Stripping back the text

Sharing written information in more succinct ways rather than the whole kitchen sink can work wonders. Some ways that you can make your written work more visually appealing, while sticking with the traditional means of application, include:

- Adding a summary section at the very beginning of your written piece, outlining the important points
- Applying dot points to allow the eye to focus on individual items
- Using short sentences

2. Interactive elements

You may get trapped into using the boring standard slide deck, but that does not mean your presentation has to be boring. You can add interactive elements that will captivate and engage your audience beyond expectations.

An example is including questions for the audience and asking 'May I see a show of hands if you…' From this, you can then speak with people in the audience and create some interaction and engagement with everyone there. It makes your presentation feel more like a personal conversation than you talking at the audience.

3. The language you use

Following on from the point above, one of the big reframes I coach people in when they're scared of getting up in front of a crowd is thinking of a presentation as a conversation rather than focusing on it being formal and very structured.

For example, instead of starting a presentation with 'Hello everyone, my name is Jo, and I am here to speak on the end-of-quarter results', try something like 'This quarter has been one of the most significant we've faced in the company's history'. This sets the context with an impressive statement that will capture your everyone's attention. Use 'you' to speak to audience members, so it feels like a one-on-one discussion.

Small language changes like this can help both you and your audience to feel more comfortable and engaged.

4. Case studies and examples

Whether it's for written or verbal communication, using case studies and real-life examples is a great way to showcase your knowledge and to throw in some creative elements. Case studies and examples also help break up some of the content you're sharing, and they provide relevant and on-point references that your audience can relate to in a memorable way. I explore using case studies further in Chapter Nine, in regard to sharing information for both left and right brain cognitive types.

Providing a visual example can be powerful and accessible – useful both for you and for those listening. Throwing in some creative elements can help transform how you communicate and share a message, even when you're stuck with the confines of company-mandated templates or you're struggling to incorporate different types of software or technology to shake things up.

Tailored information and communication

When what you're saying feels personal and targeted, people are more likely to embrace it and pay attention. Crafting your messages, your talks and your communications specifically for the audience you're speaking with is powerful.

When you see Kevin in the office, and he's charming everyone, it's because he's able to speak to people in a way that they feel connected with him. When he sees Gretel from reception, he asks her about her garden; when he speaks with Bruce from finance, they're talking about how their latest rounds of golf went. The conversations are targeted and tailored for the specific person and they're about things Kevin knows they like.

You don't need Kevin to get in the way of you having a good time.

You've done your research, so you know who you're talking to, what they're interested in and what will make them tick. Every presentation or written piece of communication is for your audience and not for you. Even though you may want it to be about things you like, you need to structure your messages so that your audience get what they will ultimately expect from the communication piece and so that they feel value from participating. You then gain the benefit of being impactful and being recognised for your important contributions.

To get the best outcome, you want your communications also to be purpose driven. Because you understand your audience, you can create a message that is based around what they need to hear. It's vital to be clear on the objective of the presentation or written piece so that the audience understands its purpose. A critical question from your audience will be *What's in it for me?* If you answer that question, you'll be providing the content that fits in with what's important and specifically relevant to them.

It's important to be mindful of language and terminology, as some things will be specific to your audience – things that wouldn't be relevant to others. We'll touch more on this in the next chapter, but I want you to consider the industry you're in, or the company you work for, and the specific words, examples or case studies that are appropriate and relevant.

The following case studies are class acts on throwing in creativity in a smart way to ensure that it follows the guidelines but reimagines how a message can be delivered.

Case studies – Netflix and Apple

For written communication

Whenever I think about an example of written communication that hits every point of being beautifully tailored for its audience, written in a clear voice, and with a clear call to action, it's a cease-and-desist letter issued by the legal team at Netflix.

CASE STUDY: Cease and desist

For those unfamiliar, in cases where it's believed a legal line has been crossed, a lawyer will send out a cease-and-desist letter to ask someone to stop doing something, stating that if that person fails to comply, legal action may be taken. The letters are usually not fun to receive. However, Netflix completely transformed how someone would view something quite negative.

It came to their attention that two ardent fans were setting up a *Stranger Things* pop-up bar – without consent. Here's an excerpt from the superbly written correspondence (for the full message, go to www.businessinsider.com/netflix-stranger-things-pop-up-bar-funny-cease-and-desist-letter-2017-9).

> '... I love how much you guys love the show. (Just wait until you see Season 2!) But unless I'm living in the Upside Down, I don't think we did a deal with you for this pop-up...
>
> We're not going to go full Dr Brenner on you, but we ask that you please (1) not extend the pop-up

beyond its 6-week run ending in September, and (2) reach out to us for permission if you plan to do something like this again.'

While the letter above is clear and lands its important message, it is delivered in a positive, fun way. If you want someone to comply with your demands, delivering the message that is outcome-focused *and* in a way that can make the recipient smile can only be a good thing.

For presentations

Apple are synonymous with creating incredible event experiences to launch their new products. Steve Jobs used his secret weapon to spread the word on these new products. The secret weapon? His messaging.

CASE STUDY: Winning tagline

The launch of the iPod in 2001 revolutionised the music world, and there was one line that helped to create and conceptualise the concept in the minds of everyone who listened.

Rather than saying something factual like 'the iPod's storage capacity is 50 megabytes', which doesn't mean much to the average person, Apple created the tagline '1000 songs in your pocket'.

People immediately understood and felt connection with this message, which transformed how they viewed the technology and how the world listened to music.

These creative methods have changed what may ordinarily be boring or uneventful to something that is captivating, engaging and fun. If you can present information in a way that captivates and transforms something in someone else's mind, you can achieve incredible results.

Engaging with stories

One of the best means of connecting with an audience and changing the way communications are received is through the power of stories.

CASE STUDY: Equal opportunities

I can remember the first conference I attended as a lawyer, in 2016. The first speaker stepped onto stage and started sharing stories of her life, leading up to the point to where she was now, as the global general counsel of a major international company and on the board of several large businesses. There was one moment that I recall above a few others, where the speaker said something along the following lines:

> 'When I was brought into the executive team, I was one of the only women at that level, and initially I felt

> like I was treated differently. ...There were subtleties such as being given the smallest office to work from, or having meetings set for times when I may want to or need to do something with my children.
>
> I felt different and I didn't want it to continue like this.
>
> Things started to change for the better, though. We got rid of our offices, and instead, all the executives were brought together to sit around a table. Altogether, bunched on this table, with our laptops and a bundle of cables running everywhere – this was the first time we were placed together as equals. I finally felt like we all had the same level playing field, we were able to have robust discussions, and we were able to have disagreements – gender didn't matter. Working together in this way meant that we didn't need to schedule meetings with each other at inconvenient times. We could discuss things there and then – it meant that I was finally an equal, and my voice was heard.'

It was a powerful story, which portrayed several visuals to consider. With the integration of stories, it helped develop what could have been a very one-dimensional discussion into an inspirational, engaging and powerful discussion. Most women could directly relate to the story, and the men in the audience could deeply think about the impact of disadvantage for their female colleagues.

For his book *Lend Me Your Ears,* Professor Max Atkinson conducted a study where he focused on an audience's reactions to certain things. He found that when a presenter said 'for example', the audience's attention was peaked – they would lift their heads, and their eyes would focus back to the presenter. This again illustrates the importance of connecting with stories as a means of thinking outside the box and adding creativity to your communications.

Relevant stories can turn an ordinary presentation into a memorable and inspirational one. As we explored in Chapter Five, you need to select your three key messages and points for your presentations. You can then highlight each key point with a story to help reinforce what you're trying to say.

If you're not balancing factual and statistical information with storytelling and other items that can engage people's brains in different ways, you will fail to capture the hearts and minds of those key people who need the information most.

Summary

Using some creative techniques in between the standard, structured ways of writing and public speaking gives your audience a fresh perspective and a transformed experience. Creativity is important in allowing your messages to land with your audience, for them to listen and take action. Your value becomes recognised because you've been able to present something in a way that is:

- Easy to read
- Tailored for the audience
- Memorable because of a story or a new way of presenting the information in a relatable way

Never let those corporate rules stop you from showing your worth with some creative techniques you can easily integrate. I'd never tell you to break the rules – what sort of lawyer would that make me? – but you can work your magic through those barriers, which will allow your audience to learn and you to shine.

PART FIVE
CONNECTION

Using our voice and words is for more than simply achieving a business outcome or making a critical point.

Our communication is also used to build trust, relationships and connection with those around us. It's the cornerstone for ensuring that when people read something you've put together, heard you speak, or joined you for a presentation, those engaging begin to know, like and trust you.

You can use your communication to connect with everyone around you.

NINE
How We Connect

The entire point of communication is to connect with others. If you're sending an email, it's to share information with someone, and it can start a longer chain of communication. If you're presenting at a conference, you want the audience to connect with you so can share your value and message with that cohort. One of the most essential factors in creating this connection is authenticity. This chapter will explore the importance of authenticity and how you can apply it in your communications.

Building connection through our communication can make a world of difference, and it gives everything a defined purpose.

Importance of authenticity

Imagine being in your company's first 'town hall' or all-company meeting of the year. The CEO, Natalie, gets in front of the room and shares a short tale from her childhood, which she somehow manages to segue into the company's objectives and targets. She walks around the stage, moving her hands expressively as she talks about the importance of reaching new customers and new countries, and how everyone needs to work together.

She pauses and approaches the front of the stage, clicks to a slide with the picture of a rainbow and says, 'This is the time. The time for everyone to go forth and create the reality we want for ourselves, this company and the world, by selling more!'

There is a gentle applause from the audience (with an overbearingly firm clap from Kevin in the front row – he really does suck, hey?).

Something about this presentation from the CEO felt a bit fake. It ticked many of the boxes a speaker and a leader should hit for a presentation, but it was somehow off the mark. The reasons for this may be hard to articulate, yet the only thing that feels like the right answer is that this presentation didn't feel *authentic*.

As explained in the *Harvard Business Review* by Nick Morgan, authenticity and the ability to communicate authentically with others is considered an important leadership skill. When leaders possess this skill, they can inspire their teams to make extraordinary efforts for the business. When they don't, employees are likely to become cynical, and people will do the bare minimum to get by.

Authenticity is considered a critical leadership attribute. In a 2023 *Forbes* article, 'Authenticity: The Key to Great Leadership and How to Embrace It', Kathy Miller Perkins says, 'Authentic leaders embrace vulnerability because they understand its power to foster trust, connection, and growth within themselves and their teams.' Communication showing this authenticity can help create a culture where there is a balance between openness and maintaining professional boundaries.

Ultimately, authenticity is about showing more of yourself and not putting up a fake persona. If what comes out of your mouth doesn't match what your body is saying, people can quickly sense that you're putting up some sort of a mask, and it will be hard for you to gain their trust.

Chris Anderson of TED Conferences said in the TED Masterclass, 'Be yourself. The worst talks are the ones where someone is trying to be someone they aren't. If someone is goofy, then be goofy; if you are emotional, be emotional.' He does also explain, though, that if someone is arrogant or self-centred, then perhaps it might be better for them to pretend to be someone else.

I love the statement above because when you're yourself, and you are comfortable sharing and communicating as yourself, you step into a new level of appearing confident. It allows you to connect more easily with the audiences who are watching because they can see what you're like, how you speak and your general vibe.

You can still be authentic and adapt to the situations you're in. You don't speak the same way in the bar as you would in the boardroom. As humans, we're chameleons – we can adapt and change based on the situation we're in, and as we looked at earlier, sometimes it's important to tailor your communication for the particular audience. You can do that in a way that is still authentic and true to who you are, though, without seeming like a fake snake. Your authenticity and truth when communicating will win others over more than any Oscar-winning performance. When someone seems too polished, or where their words don't match their body language, they lose touch with those that are listening, and the trust begins to dissolve.

Our communication can and should be used to connect, and there are some handy techniques that can be applied to create that connection.

Aristotle's approach to communication

As a Greek person, I feel proud that one of the greatest philosophers of all times, Aristotle, developed an approach that can transform your communication.

The Rhetoric Triangle uses components that you may not have purposely considered for your written and verbal communication, but you may incidentally apply some of them because of how important they are.

Aristotle taught us that a speaker's ability to persuade an audience was based on how well a speaker can appeal to an audience through three different areas: logos, ethos and pathos. Combined, this is known as the Rhetoric Triangle. To ensure you understand the three points of the triangle, I'll outline each in some detail:

1. **Logos:** Related to the term 'logic' in English, logos is about how you can appeal to reason. Where a communicator relies on logos, they are utilising facts, data and statistics to support an argument or point. This instils credibility because it's clear you have conducted research and work to substantiate your authority on the matter.
2. **Ethos:** This translates from Greek and refers to habit, custom or character. In the Rhetoric Triangle, ethos refers to the appeal to credibility or authority. It's about how you write or how you carry yourself on stage and in front of an audience – your voice, enthusiasm, language and authenticity. This is where your preparation, research and presentation skills kick into gear. Do you sound like you genuinely support and care what you're talking about? Do you have the

experience and understanding to be presenting on this topic or writing this report?

3. **Pathos:** This is the appeal to emotion. Aristotle used pathos to refer to the emotional impact that communications can have on an audience. In communication, the language and stories you use should aim to create an emotional reaction. It's all about how you want your audience to feel – they will be more likely to listen and take action if they feel moved by what you've articulated. The Rhetoric Triangle is another tool for your communication toolkit, useful when you are putting any content together. It combines the logical aspects, your authority as a communicator and how you want the audience to feel, to inspire action. These aspects all assist with building that connection with your audience as they begin to feel what you're saying and trust you as the person saying it.

Left brain vs right brain – reaching and connecting with everyone

Your audience will interpret information differently and you can assist in providing a breadth of material which will appeal to everyone in the room. As Ann Pietrangelo explains in a *Healthline* article, the brain is a complex and complicated organ that contains up to 100 billion neurons and trillions of connections. It is divided into two hemispheres, with each processing information differently.

A way of considering how you position the material you present could be based on left brain or right brain orientation. Left brain focused content is more analytical and methodical, while right brain focused material may be more creative and artistic. When you prepare content, you should ensure that each point speaks to balancing both left brain and right brain characteristics.

Doing this effectively will mean you are thinking about everything from a left brain versus right brain perspective, enabling your content to connect in different ways. You want to share messages that can dance across the spectrum of left brain logic through to right brain creativity, allowing everyone in the audience to walk away feeling you've connected with them and that they can take something powerful away from your communication.

Left brain characteristics

The left side is often associated with logical thinking, analysis and language skills. Tips to position content to favour left brain include:

- **Organise information logically:** Structure your presentation in a clear and coherent manner.

Having a clear and logical structure helps your left brain pals know where you're heading in the presentation.

- **Provide data and evidence:** Support your key message with facts, statistics and logical reasoning. Use charts, graphs and visuals to present data effectively.
- **Use precise language:** Be clear and concise in your explanations. Being methodical and straight up with how you share information will be appreciated. Of course, using those important plain English principles will do you wonders.
- **Encourage critical thinking:** Pose questions, present problems and engage the audience in analytical thinking to stimulate their left brain activity.

Right brain characteristics

The right brain is associated with creativity, visualisation and holistic thinking. Techniques that will help position right brain focused information for your audience include:

- **Use visual aids:** Include images, videos and diagrams that help convey your message visually and stimulate the audience's imagination. Where you've used some statistics and facts for your left brain friends, follow these up with an image for your right brain audience members.

- **Tell stories:** Include narratives and anecdotes to engage the audience emotionally and make your presentation more memorable. As we know, storytelling can help to connect and creatively share information with your audience.
- **Incorporate creativity:** Use metaphors, analogies and creative visuals to present complex concepts or ideas. You can also allow for open-ended thinking and encourage brainstorming during your presentation – those interactive elements can help create different thinking.
- **Create a visually appealing presentation:** Pay attention to the design, colour scheme and layout of your slides. Aesthetically pleasing visuals can enhance the overall impact (and too much text is simply a no-no).

Speaking a language others can understand

As much as Kevin can get on our nerves, there is something he is really good at: being able to connect with everyone at work. He'll just bounce around with a coffee in hand, having chats with different people about all sorts of things. You don't know what he's chatting to all those people about, but they're clearly having a great time.

What is he doing that is so effective? He is speaking in the specific language of those people – whether it's the tailored language of industry professionals, terminology you'd only hear in a particular team, or language that is only applicable to the type of business you're in or the type of person you're engaging with.

Sheida A Rad, an executive language coach, highlights in a 2023 LinkedIn article that having a strong grasp of industry-specific language can be beneficial for career development. It can demonstrate your expertise and knowledge in a specific field, and familiarity with the language used in other industries and teams can show that you understand those people.

I'll explain different categories to help conceptualise what I mean about these other languages and how they can be used to build connection and trust, so you know where you can focus.

Industry-specific terminology

You can focus on a particular industry that you or your audience are a part of. It could be specific such as real estate, insurance or law; or it could be more general such as technology, start-ups or business. If, for example, you're talking to someone who is an expert at real estate, you could throw in things such as easement (where someone has the right to use the land of another), or the BCA (Building Code of Australia), where these things are relevant and in context with the conversation.

Company/business-specific terminology

Different companies and types of businesses often have their own language. For example, in the university sector VC stands for vice chancellor, while in the start-up space it means venture capital – obviously two very different things. In the tech companies I've worked for, terms such as SaaS (software as a service) were particularly common, while financial terms such as ARR (annual recurring revenue) or churn rate (percentage of paying customers who cancel their product) were less common but it was assumed those who worked in this fast-moving space were familiar with the terms.

When I first entered a new industry, I had to learn so many new terms. If I didn't know them, I felt a little silly, but it wasn't long before I understood everything I needed to. It was the same when I worked with different teams and presented to them. If I didn't fully understand what people were saying, I'd have a very tricky time working with them, and it would be difficult for me to gain their trust.

CASE STUDY: Working with different business units

As an in-house lawyer, I regularly needed to conduct internal training to ensure people were aware of the legal issues they may face in their departments and what they could personally do without necessarily needing to seek legal help.

I recall a time where I needed to do work with the marketing department, who were sending me a heap of little requests about things that weren't particularly risky issues. I wanted to be able to support them but not have to be there to hold their hand every time they needed something.

I decided the best way forward would be to create some tools for them to use and then conduct some training to help improve their knowledge. When putting the training together, I had to think about the examples I used and the way I explained things, as I needed to ensure I didn't bore them and that I communicated these complicated concepts in a language they would understand. Here are some of the tactics I used:

- It's vital to obtain consent from the people being photographed and interviewed, to ensure they're happy for it to be published online. That consent is normally recorded on a form called a 'personal information consent' form, which is a little bit sterile. I decided to rename it as the 'talent release form' – something my marketing friends would understand and be familiar with. Speaking in the language they understood made it clear that I understood what they needed and how I could assist them.
- When exploring stories to use in the training, I used examples from their day-to-day world, including situations I assisted with and events they were part of. This allowed me to build that connection I needed.

I needed to include sufficient factual information, some data and statistics in my training, and also back that up with stories, images and real-life case studies to show the impacts in real life to ensure that my material catered to both the left and right brain characteristics of my colleagues.

Summary

Communication without connection is almost pointless. When you communicate, you must show your authentic self to allow people to get to know you and why you're on stage. Aristotle has also shown us that communication can create an emotional connection, which is important to show our credibility, and that there must be proof of logic in what you say. Together, these three elements are important for building a connection with your audience.

This chapter explored the concept of creating content that hits both left brain and right brain focused content, as you want everyone in your audience to feel you're speaking to them, which will strengthen your connection with them. To further establish a connection, speaking to others in ways they understand, using industry-specific terminology, shows that you understand them.

You have the potential to influence others, be impactful, and make a real difference every time you speak. Creating a connection will only support that and boost your potential moving forward.

TEN

Using Our Communication Right

Having a voice and a platform is incredible and something that shouldn't be taken for granted. Whatever your environment, there are captive audiences who can be influenced by what you have to say. If you're reading this book, there is a strong chance you also want to improve how influential you can be and to be well equipped to make some moves.

Creating a connection and a feeling of trust is an important part of making a lasting impression. This chapter explains why it's so important for you to establish trust and keep building it to create lasting impressions when you're on stage, in a virtual meeting or putting a written piece of work together. Your audiences and colleagues need to know, like and trust you before they will listen to what you're saying.

Why do we need to establish trust?

I get asked to join a lot of sales calls and demos where I'm not the person selling – I am the person being sold to. Whether it's in the legal world – where I have tech vendors trying to sell me legal tech software – or whether its business coaches wanting to share how I can become a '15-figure entrepreneur', these people see me as a cheque book. Almost every time I join these calls (often through a digital platform like Zoom or Google Meets), I hear about thirty seconds of filler content such as 'How is the weather where you are?' before we get right into trying to hustle.

Usually before joining, I get asked to complete a pre-meeting questionnaire, asking about my needs, goals, frustrations and everything in between to ensure I'm the sort of customer they're looking for. Somehow, though, the person I'm speaking to is asking me the same questions, as if they've completely ignored the fact that information was available a week in advance.

The red flags continue. The conversation almost always turns to emotional turmoil, making me feel bad about myself, with the salesperson trying to convince me that their solution/service/dishwashing liquid is the only thing that would ever make my life better. I found these conversations infuriating. It's one of the things that most inspired me to write this book, to share important lessons for your communication, public speaking and presentation skills.

Your communication can be used in so many different ways, and you should always consider how people feel when you deliver your message.

These salespeople are trying hard but failing at a few things:

- They don't get to know me and act as if they know nothing about me.
- They don't present to me as if they knew who their audience is (the calls feel very generic and forced).
- They push their products onto me.
- They don't do anything to establish a level of trust with me.

In marketing, they often refer to a powerful technique as the Know, Like, Trust mentality:

1. **Know:** The person grows their understanding about you. They know about you, your industry and the things that are important.
2. **Like:** This requires the salesperson to be authentic and relatable, and to establish a connection with you.
3. **Trust:** This is built through showing transparency, demonstrating that there is a level of honesty and maybe some vulnerability, and of course showing some level of authority and credibility through expressing knowledge and experience.

Joseph Folkman explained in a *Forbes* article that after conducting a study of over 97,000 leaders who had been evaluated by their direct reports (which were over 509,000 people), the leaders who were most trusted and had good communication skills were ranked much higher, with ratings entering the sixtieth percentile. He explained:

> 'Trust is the leverage you have to communicate well or to be ignored. As you attempt to communicate with others ask yourself the questions "Do they trust me?" "What can I do to increase my trust?" "Is there something I am promising that might cause them to lose trust in me?"'

When you step onto a stage, or when you want people to listen to what you're saying in an email, trust allows you to be listened to. You can be influential because you've created a level of trust where someone wants to listen and engage with you. I know that, in my job as a lawyer, if people don't trust what I have to say, no one will listen, and my job will be in jeopardy. When I step on stage, I want the audience to feel they can know me, like me and trust me. I therefore create levels of connection by:

- Showing I understand their frustrations
- Demonstrating some vulnerability about things I've struggled with

- Manifesting my credibility by explaining the research and work I've done

To show how you can build trust further, I'm sharing the following work from a TED Talk that I watch regularly.

The Trust Triangle

One of my all-time favourite TED Talks is *How to build (and rebuild) trust* by Frances Frei of Harvard University. Her talk explores the component parts of trust, which she distinguishes as:

1. If you sense that someone is being authentic, you're more likely to trust them.
2. If you sense that there is rigour in someone's logic, you are more likely to trust them.
3. If you believe someone's empathy is directed towards you, you are more likely to trust them.

When all three of these elements are working together, there is trust. When one of the limbs is broken, trust can be threatened.

You want to make sure that there is always enough trust between you and the people you're speaking with for the sake of being the credible authority that others want to come to in the workplace and in life generally. Frances goes into how to deal with trust threats, which I'll refer to, providing also my own insights into how you can create trust in your communications.

Authenticity

Being authentic is twofold – you want to appear authentic to create trust and connection (as covered in Chapter Nine), but you also need to be able to be authentic and feel safe to be yourself, for your own purposes.

You want to balance how you speak, present, share and write information in a way that is true to you and also incorporates things that are necessary for the business or the environment you're communicating in. People connect with people, so showing some levels of vulnerability, humour and your personality when presenting will go a long way in how others connect with you and understand you.

The threat is that you may not feel comfortable to be 'all in' as yourself, and you may feel a bit guarded. This is normal because it can feel risky. Once you can put your armour down, you may find a level of connection with others you may not have envisaged. Showing up as yourself and bringing your personality will only win more favours with your audiences.

Logic

You need to be the authority to speak and communicate, and I've provided the tools for you to show your credibility and authority through your experience and education.

Frei says that when we speak, we often like to share plenty of detail, taking our listeners on a journey of twists and turns. The danger here is you can get interrupted and not end up making the point you want. Frei recommends making your point or statement first, and then provide the supporting material to back it up.

This is similar to the approach I've mentioned earlier, where you start by deciding on your key message. To make sure that message is heard, you create three key points that support it and illustrate it. Finally, in each of those three points, you use left brain and right brain material to capture everyone in your audience.

Empathy

The most common trust failure is empathy. Frei outlines that this failure appears where people don't feel that others are in it for them, instead believing that others are too self-distracted. She says, 'We are all so busy with so many demands on our time, it's easy to crowd out the time and space that empathy requires.'

One of the best means of showing your empathy is to give someone your attention. As a communicator, it is critical you truly listen to what you're being told, giving the other person the space to talk. Particularly in the professional services space, or if you're in sales, much of the role requires you to listen to what your clients and colleagues want and need. When you're speaking on stage or sharing information in a report, although it's an opportunity to share what you know, it's critical that you use that opportunity to help solve the problem the person was asking about, and to provide value to the audience. You need initially to have listened and considered what will make this an important and considered communication piece for your audience. When preparing that communication, you need to use empathy to have your audience at the front of your mind.

Without trust, you cannot build connections and have the influence you'd like to. Applying the elements of the Trust Triangle will enable you to become a trusted communicator, allowing you to make a significant impact every time you interact with others. It is important to consider the potential impact of what you're communicating, and why establishing and creating a positive connection is so important.

Empathy as a communicator

In her industry blog, Amy Boone at Ethos3 explains:

> 'What does empathy have to do with giving a presentation? More than you might think. Empathy is a crucial component of human connection. And when it comes to communication, it can remind us that presentations work best when they are developed with the audience in mind.'

You can show empathy by demonstrating that you have an understanding about how your audience may feel in certain circumstances or even assuming what they may be thinking. You could say something like 'You might be thinking…' to show that you know that those listening may think you're a little crazy in what you're saying, but you're about to convince them otherwise. It shows you understand their thought process.

Being empathetic may come more easily to some than others, but one of the big myths I want to bust is that your personality type doesn't define whether you're a good communicator or presenter. Extroversion is often characterised by traits such as sociability and enjoying being the centre of attention. Extroverts also enjoy social settings and feel energised interacting with others. Introverts, on the other hand, tend to be more reserved and keep their emotional states private. Olivia Guy-Evans, MSc, at Simply Psychology, explains that introverts feel more comfortable in and get their energy from lower-stimulus environments.

Extroverts are going to be more confident to step onto the stage, while our introverted friends are more likely to worry about what the audience thinks and feels; it is common that they will naturally have more empathy. As reported in a 2016 *Business Insider* article (Richard Feloni), Dananjaya Hettiarachchi, a champion public speaker, believes that 'introverts excel as public speakers when, through practice, they identify with the audience and "connect with them on a deeper level" than extroverts, who often project themselves onto their audience'.

Applying a level of empathy when you present information to an audience will provide you more opportunity to connect and develop a relationship of trust with those in the room. Anyone can do this, even though it might come more easily to introverts.

The Karen and how not to communicate

During the early days of the pandemic, I wrote a blog post titled 'The Rise of the Karens' with the lens that the media was using, focusing on this figure causing drama everywhere she went. For those unfamiliar with the term, the 'Karen' stereotype is a middle-class white woman, with a bob-style haircut, who argues unreasonably with anyone who displeases her. In her home, meanwhile, she may have a 'Live, Laugh, Love' decal in the kitchen.

When this stereotype emerged, videos began filling social media platforms and local media channels, showing Karen-type figures causing fights with 'suspicious' people parking to close to her home, or being rude to service personnel in the supermarket, or even being abusive to waiters at coffee shops. These videos demonstrated the aggressive nature of the Karen stereotype and her male equivalent, 'David'. My blog post centred around the fact that individuals have a voice and should use it for positive things rather than degrading others and causing more hurt, particularly during a difficult period.

When I think about communication and how important it is to consider it as a service, 'Karen' is certainly the opposite of my ideal audience member. I do think it's important to know what not to do, and I therefore use the 'Karen' stereotype as an opportunity to reflect and improve. There are two main reasons – other than the obvious ones such as aggression, racism and rudeness – that makes this type of person an ineffective communicator who is unlikely to build a connection.

1. **Assuming others understand you**

   Karen is at the café and asks for her coffee 'the way I normally like it', but when it arrives, it is a normal heat instead of the scalding coffee her regular barista makes for her. She then, of course, blasts the barista for not knowing what her expectations are.

   This is something you may do in your presentations, if you start talking about concepts your audience may not understand or aren't familiar with. You can never assume that your audience knows what you're saying, and you need to ensure that what you're delivering is what they're expecting.

2. **Talking instead of engaging**

   You can't just stand there and talk at people unless perhaps you're delivering a lecture, when people often just sit and listen for the purpose of learning. When you're looking to use your public speaking skills as a means of captivating an audience and using it to share an influential message, you want your audience to be engaged and an active part of it.

   As highlighted earlier, you should aim to make your presentation like a conversation so that it feels less structured and more natural. Using engagement techniques such as audience interaction and live polling will make your listeners feel they are part of the experience and not a potato.

A lot can be said for the skill of listening. This is of course linked to listening to what your audience wants, and the things that are of interest or importance to them, increasing your chances of connecting with them.

Implementing active listening as part of your emotional skills could be a game changer. A 2018 paper by McKinsey (Bughin), reports that the demand for social and emotional skills is projected to grow by more than 20% across all industries from 2016 until 2030.

With all of this combined, it's important to remember that your voice is powerful and shouldn't be taken for granted. If you are given the opportunity to share a message and leave people feeling something new, make sure your message is helpful and something you can be proud of.

Summary

Establishing a connection is important, and the best way to do that is through building trust. Understanding the elements of the Trust Triangle – authenticity, logic and empathy – and knowing what to do when any of those are compromised, can assist in building levels of trust to lead to connection.

When learning to build a connection with your public speaking and communication skills, it's also important to know what not to do. The Karen stereotype is definitely not a good representation of how to build trust and connection. If anything, it gives good examples of what you shouldn't be doing.

Empathy is a tool you should add to your collection, realising that this skill allows you to understand the hearts and minds of your audience, which enables you to create a piece of communication that is perfect for them.

Conclusion

Your ability to communicate is one of the most powerful tools you have. Being able to effectively use your voice will allow you to be valued and understood by those around you because they can hear and understand the critical things that you have to say.

I want you to be empowered, comfortable and happy to stand up in front of the boardroom, when you unmute your microphone on Zoom, or when you hit send on that email. Your value and your worth are clear, and you can broadcast that through your communication.

Over the five parts of this book, I've taken you on a journey through my 5C methodology for crafting and delivering messages that matter. The 5C principles are:

1. Clarity
2. Conciseness
3. Confidence
4. Creativity
5. Connection

Combining these principles gives you the best way to think about, prepare for and deliver your messages, regardless of the communication method.

With my background as a corporate lawyer, TEDx speaker and TEDx licensee and director, I've wanted to bring you the lessons and anecdotes that have impacted me most, including what I've seen and learned from TED Talks, to allow you to succeed in your role. I understand the challenges that most people face, and I want to enable you to fight those difficulties and smash through them.

Being influential in your communication can help propel your career forward. Being able to use your voice and words to communicate a message to your most important stakeholders in a way they understand, which feels like it's made specifically for them and that answers their burning questions, can enable you to demonstrate your value and worth as a contributor.

There is always more work that can be done. Communication skills require continual fine tuning, attention and work – this will never be a one and done achievement.

The fact you're reading this book proves you've recognised the need to improve, and if there's anything you'd like to do after reading this, I'd be keen to work with you. I have a range of programmes available on my website, including free resources, an online on-demand course, coaching programmes, and speaking and workshop opportunities. Check me out at www.theokap.com.au.

This is your opportunity to speak up, show up and make an impact with your voice and words. You now have the opportunity to rock this world with your messages that matter.

References

Abrahams, M, 'One Communication Tool You Should Add to Your Toolkit', Stanford Graduate School of Business (4 January 2017), www.gsb.stanford.edu/insights/one-communication-tool-you-should-add-your-toolkit, accessed 18 March 2024

Anderson, C, *TED Talks: The Official TED Guide to Public Speaking* (Hodder and Stoughton, 2016)

Anderson, C, Course Preview, TED Masterclass, https://mastercle-overview, accessed 9 April 2024

Andy L, 'Read These Humorous COVID-19 Digital Ads by Coronavirus.gov', Muse.World (14 April 2020), https://muse.world/read-these-humorous-covid-19-digital-ads-by-coronavirus-gov, accessed 19 March 2024

Atkinson, M, *Lend Me Your Ears: All You Need to Know About Making Speeches and Presentations* (Vermilion, 2004)

Barnard, D, 'Average Speaking Rate and Words per Minute', VirtualSpeech (8 November 2022), https://virtualspeech.com/blog/average-speaking-rate-words-per-minute, accessed 8 April 2024

Boone, A, '2 Phrases That Infuse a Presentation with Empathy', Ethos3, https://ethos3.com/2-phrases-that-infuse-a-presentation-with-empathy, accessed 21 March 2024

Brown, B, *Dare to Lead: Brave Work. Tough Conversations. Whole Hearts.* (Vermilion, 2018)

Brown, B, *The Power of Vulnerability* (TED Talk, June 2010), www.ted.com/talks/brene_brown_the_power_of_vulnerability, accessed 20 March 2024

Bughin, J, et al, 'Skill Shift: Automation and the Future of the Workforce', McKinsey & Company (23 May 2018), www.mckinsey.com/featured-insights/future-of-work/skill-shift-automation-and-the-future-of-the-workforce, accessed 21 March 2024

Cartwright, J, '17 PowerPoint Presentation Tips to Make More Creative Slideshows [+ Templates]', HubSpot (16 August 2023), https://blog.hubspot.com/marketing/easy-powerpoint-design-tricks-ht, accessed 18 March 2024

Codrea-Rado, A, 'I Sent Voice Messages Instead of Emails and Started Landing Better-Paying Work. It's

How I Plan to Pitch for New Work From Now On', *Business Insider* (29 September 2022), www.businessinsider.com/gmail-voice-note-email-pitching-for-work-freelancer-voice-memo-2022-9, accessed 19 March 2024

DuCharme, KA, and Brawley, LR, 'Predicting the intentions and behavior of exercise initiates using two forms of self-efficacy', *Journal of Behavioral Medicine, 18/5* (1995), 479–497, doi: 10.1007/BF01904775

Feloni, R, 'A world champion public speaker says introverts often make better speakers than extroverts', *Business Insider* (21 May 2016), www.businessinsider.com/champion-public-speaker-says-introverts-can-make-better-speakers-2016-5, accessed 9 May 2024

Folkman, J, 'How Trust Affects Your Ability to Communicate and How to Fix It', *Forbes* (7 April 2020), www.forbes.com/sites/joefolkman/2020/04/07/how-trust-effects-your-ability-to-communicate-and-how-to-fix-it, accessed 21 March 2024

Frei, F, *How to Build (and Rebuild) Trust* (TED Talk, April 2018), www.ted.com/talks/frances_frei_how_to_build_and_rebuild_trust, accessed 20 March 2024

Guy-Evans, O, 'Introvert Vs. Extrovert Personality: Signs, Theories, and Differences', Simply Psychology (29 January 2024), www.simplypsychology.org/introvert-extrovert.html, accessed 21 March 2024

Kapodistrias, T, *Lessons From My Ethnic Lunchbox* (TED Talk, 30 June 2023), www.youtube.com/watch?v=WG4JGm6nUDM&t=247s, accessed 21 March 2024

McCarraher, L and Gregory, J, *Bookbuilder: The Definitive Guide to Writing the Book to Transform Your Business* (Rethink Press, 2020)

McKerihan, S, *Clear and Concise: Become a Better Business Writer* (Schwartz Publishing Pty Ltd, 2015)

McNamara, B, 'The Science Behind Social Media's Hold on Our Mental Health', *teenVogue* (10 November 2021), www.teenvogue.com/story/the-science-behind-social-medias-hold-on-our-mental-health, accessed 11 April 2024

Medical News Today, 'What Is Box Breathing?' (19 October 2023), www.medicalnewstoday.com/articles/321805, accessed 18 March 2024

Morgan, N, 'How to Become an Authentic Speaker', *Harvard Business Review* (November 2008), https://hbr.org/2008/11/how-to-become-an-authentic-speaker, accessed 19 March 2024

Morley, M, 'Tupperware Was the Original Social Network of 1950s Suburbia', *Eye on Design* (July 2019), www.madeleine-morley.com/writing/tupperware, accessed 15 March 2024

Nelson, DL, Reed, V and Walling, JR, 'The Pictorial Superiority Effect', *Journal of Experimental Psychology: Human Learning and Memory*, 2 (1976), 523–528

Pala, S, 'Why It's Important to Have an Emotional Connection With Your Audience', *Inc.* (11 Jan 2019), www.inc.com / serhat-pala / 3-ways-to-use-emotion-to-connect-to-your-audience.html, accessed 10 May 2024

Perkins, KM, 'Authenticity: The Key to Great Leadership and How to Embrace It', *Forbes* (27 May 2023), www.forbes.com / sites / kathymillerperkins / 2023 / 05 / 27 / authenticity-the-key-to-great-leadership-and-how-to-embrace-it / ?sh=f88bcc02050e, accessed 10 April 2024

Pietrangelo, A, 'Left Brain vs. Right Brain: What Does This Mean for Me?', *Healthline* (5 February 2024), www.healthline.com / health / left-brain-vs-right-brain, accessed 21 March 2024

Priestley, D, *Key Person of Influence: The Five-Step Method to Become One of the Most Highly Valued and Highly Paid People in Your Industry* (Rethink Press, 2014)

PwC Australia, 'The Power of Visual Communication: Showing Your Story to Land the Message', PwC Australia Comms Lab (April 2017), www.pwc.com.au / the-difference / the-power-of-visual-communication-apr17.pdf, accessed 19 March 2024

Rad, SA, 'The Power of Industry-Specific Language in Career Advancement', LinkedIn (23 February 2023), www.linkedin.com / pulse / power-industry-specific-language-career-advancement-sheida-a-rad, accessed 20 March 2024

Russell, C, *'Looks Aren't Everything. Believe Me, I'm a Model'* (TED Talk, January 2013), www.ted.com/talks/cameron_russell_looks_aren_t_everything_believe_me_i_m_a_model, accessed 20 March 2024

Song, H and Schwarz, N, 'If It's Hard to Read, It's Hard to Do: Processing fluency affects effort prediction and motivation', *Psychological Science,* 19 (2008), 986–988, https://journals.sagepub.com/doi/abs/10.1111/j.1467-9280.2008.02189.x

Sparks, P, Guthrie, CA, and Shepherd, R, 'The dimensional structure of the perceived behavioral control construct', *Journal of Applied Social Psychology, 27/5* (1997), 418–438, https://doi.org/10.1111/j.1559-1816.1997.tb00639.x

Terrell Hanna, K, 'DEFINITION: Infographic', TechTarget, www.techtarget.com/whatis/definition/infographics, accessed 19 March 2024

The Coaching Room, '"Just": One Word That Undermines You Daily and How to Change It', https://thecoachingroom.com.au/blog/just-one-word-that-undermines-you-daily-and-how-to-change-it, accessed 27 April 2024

Urban, T, *'Inside the Mind of a Master Procrastinator'*, (TED Talk, February 2016), https://www.ted.com/talks/tim_urban_inside_the_mind_of_a_master_procrastinator, accessed 27 April 2024

Urban, T, Wait But Why, Blog, https://waitbutwhy.com, accessed 11 April 2024

Acknowledgements

This book has certainly been a journey for me. I started it in the week of my first TEDxHobart event, and I struggled then to imagine it ever being completed. I am so proud that I've been able to finish it and will be able see it out into the world.

Projects like this don't just happen. They require everyone around you to support your writing and to assist you through the entire process.

I'd like to thank my family, in particular my mum, dad and brother, for their constant support, and for their surprise every time I announce something new that I'm doing. Without their encouragement, it would be hard to keep going with these difficult endeavours.

I'd like to thank all of my friends for checking in, keeping me accountable and pushing me to finish the manuscript.

Some of my oldest and closet friends, near and far, thank you for always being by my side. In particular: Sam, Maddie and Liz, who have known me forever; all of my incredible friends in the tourism space; my legal legend friends; my quiz night and activities friends; my awesome friends in the WOTSO co-working space; and of course, all of my colleagues, who I've had the joy to work with over the years. There are too many of you to name personally, but you know who you are.

Someone who no longer lives near me but still gets a bucketload of me complaining is Matt ('Forni') Fornaciari. Thanks for agreeing to write my foreword and for teaching me the importance of speaking kindly to myself.

I'd finally like to thank the wonderful people at Rethink Press for their work in helping to bring this book to life!

I cannot wait to see this book making a huge impact and change in the world.

Thank you for investing in it, and I hope you enjoy it for years to come.

The Author

Theo Kapodistrias is a multi-award-winning lawyer and communications expert, based in Hobart, Tasmania. He is also an award-winning speaker, trainer and MC, and a public speaking, presentations and communication coach, running his own business: www.theokap.com.au.

Theo has been recognised, winning several awards, for his work in the legal and community space. He was named as one of Australia's most influential lawyers by the *Australasian Lawyer* magazine in both 2022 and 2023. In 2022 he was recognised as International Speaker of the Year at the International Coaches

Awards, and in 2023 he was named as one of the leading speech coaches in Australia and New Zealand, according to Yoodli.

He uses his legal, governance and communication skills for good and has held non-executive director roles with the Association of Corporate Counsel (ACC) Australia and with Business Events Tasmania. With ACC Australia, he is also the Tasmanian divisional president and chair of the Sole Legal Officer Special Interest Group.

In 2021 Theo became executive director and licensee of TEDxHobart, and he is the host of the *Craft Messages That Matter* podcast. In 2023 he also become a TEDx speaker presenting at TEDxKatoomba, with his talk *Lessons from my ethnic lunchbox*, which has attracted over 20,000 views on YouTube.

Find Theo Kapodistrias:

www.theokap.com.au

www.instagram.com / @theokap88

@theokap88

www.facebook.com / theokap.com.au

www.linkedin.com / in / theo-kapodistrias

www.ingramcontent.com/pod-product-compliance
Lightning Source LLC
Chambersburg PA
CBHW071548200326
41519CB00021BB/6659
* 9 7 8 1 7 8 1 3 3 8 6 7 4 *